AN INTRODU
3D MOVEMENTS

EMPOWERING
MISSIONAL
DISCIPLES

BOB ROGNLIEN

3DM Publishing

3dmpublishing.com

CONTENTS

DEDICATION

To Mike and Sally Breen
who invited us into their *oikos*,
taught us how to disciple leaders,
and showed us what it means to be spiritual parents.
We are so grateful.

ACKNOWLEDGEMENTS

The core teachings and tools contained in this book were taught to me and modeled for me by Mike Breen, founder of the discipling and missional movement to which this is an introduction. The organization, articulation, and contextualization of these teachings and tools is my own.

I want to express my deepest thanks to the many amazing leaders who have gone with me on this journey of discipleship and mission over the past eight years. You have become our spiritual family. It has not always been easy, but it has always been worth it!

I also want to thank those who made the publication of this book possible: Pam Rognlien for reading and improving its many drafts; Jerry McSwain for giving thorough and valuable input; Robert Neely for his excellent editing; Libby Culmer for making it all happen behind the scenes; and Blake Berg for his inspired design.

Above all, I want to thank my beloved Pamela for faithfully walking this path with me for thirty years, and Bobby, Amy, Luke, and Taylor for being not only our biological family, but the heart of our spiritual family as well. Thank you, Jesus, for this incredible gift! My cup overflows...

FOREWORD

By Mike Breen

Jesus said that his objective and his expectation for his disciples was that they would do greater things than he had done. For us this seems almost unimaginable. How could his disciples have a greater impact on the people with whom they met? How could the things that they did be of greater power and significance than raising Lazarus from the dead? Nevertheless, this was his expectation, and given the growth, scope, and impact of the church—which today forms the cultural backdrop to one-third of the world's population and daily sees the miraculous transformation of thousands of lives—who can suggest that his expectations were not fulfilled?

As discipling leaders we long to develop disciples of Jesus who, in following us, do more than we could ever do. Bob Rognlien is such a disciple. Bob's commitment–and that of his wife Pam–to building a "discipling culture" and forming a "family on mission" have been exemplary. His loyalty, integrity, and consistency are an example to us all. And now he has written a book that exceeds anything that I as his discipling leader could have written!

Bob takes the now familiar content of the 3DM discipling movement and applies it to the contemporary experience of the many pastors and leaders with whom he has worked. He tells his own story and offers trenchant and insightful commentary of how to implement change and growth.

His overview of the causes and problems the Western church faces as it tries to make disciples is tremendously helpful and insightful, and his remedies and solutions are both compelling and eminently doable. As you dive into the material, you will find answers to the two big questions facing leaders wrestling with the subject. Why do we find it so difficult to make disciples? And how, faced with all these difficulties, we can still achieve our aim?

If you're a leader desiring to multiply the life of Jesus in those whom you lead, and if you want to be a leader whose disciples do greater things than you have done, then this is the book for you.

INTRODUCTION

JESUS' CHURCH VS. OUR CHURCH

1

JOINING A MOVEMENT

THE RIGHT STUFF

I love to build things. When I was a kid, Legos™ were my best friend.
I spent untold hours creating outlandish spacecraft or impossibly complex mansions—you know, the kind where James Bond's nemesis plots his
world domination. Legos™ are great, except when you don't have the right
pieces. Sometimes I had a vision for what I wanted to build, but I didn't
have the building blocks to enable me to make the vision a reality.

As I got older, my building projects moved to the barn (because we didn't
have a garage). I would look around at the scrap lumber and my dad's
tool bench and start to create a masterpiece. It usually involved a ramp
to launch my bike into space or a project "beautifying" our little ranch
in some way. Inevitably my creativity bumped up against the limitations
of tools and materials. "Where can a guy get an arc welder around here?
Anyone seen a small rocket engine lying around?"

In college I worked sum-
mers for a contractor,
framing houses. I loved
to watch a bare founda-
tion and a pile of 2x4s
steadily take the shape of
a new home. One thing
I discovered about successful contractors is that they always had the tools
and materials needed to complete the job. Just as Jesus' parable about building a tower teaches (Luke 14:28), they sat down well ahead of time, pored
over the blueprints, and carefully determined exactly the tools, personnel,
lumber, and hardware needed to make the plans a reality. It's incredibly
frustrating when you need 12-foot 2x8s to frame a roof, but all you have
are 8 footers. And nothing is worse than trying to pound a 16 penny nail
with a Phillips head screwdriver, or trying to pull out that same nail with a
pair of pliers! Once you have the right tools and the right materials, however, it's amazing what you can accomplish. At that point all you need is
the knowhow.

You don't go to school to learn how to build a house—you join a crew. You
need practical knowledge and skills. When I first started working in construction, my boss paired me with an experienced carpenter for on-the-job
training. Sometimes my mentor would explain how to lay out the plates
for framing a wall or how to use a speed square to mark the angle for the
end cut on a rafter. Other times I learned how to do it by watching what
he did and imitating him. I will never forget watching this master builder
use a slide square to put a parallel pencil line along the edge of a board. I
only had to see him do it once, and for the rest of my life I have known
how to do it. By the time I was in graduate school, I was the foreman running the job because I knew how to frame an entire custom home from
start to finish.

WHAT ARE YOU BUILDING?

God is the ultimate architect. He has the most amazing set of blueprints that describe the life for which you were created. Jesus is the sure foundation of that building, and the Holy Spirit is ready to lead you in constructing that life. As Paul said to the Corinthians, *According to the grace of God given to me, like a skilled master builder I laid a foundation, and someone else is building upon it. Let each one take care how he builds upon it.* (1 Corinthians 3:10)

How are you building on that foundation? Do you have the materials you need? Do you have the tools required? Is there someone in your life more experienced than you showing you how to do it?

We are all building something. But we have to ask ourselves if we are building what God has created us to build. Do our lives reflect the Father's design? Before I could become God's builder, I had to come to the realization that I did not have the tools or the knowhow to build the life God had designed for me.

I came to faith in Jesus Christ as a high school student. I was blessed with a great pastor and a devoted youth minister who invited me to be a part of the ministries they were leading. As I got involved in church leadership as a young man, I began to notice that I was an exception to the rule. Most people in our church simply came on Sunday to attend the worship service, placed an offering in the plate as it passed by, and chatted with friends over coffee afterward. I could tell this frustrated my pastor, and he worked hard to get people more involved. Some responded, but most did not. It was as if there was some kind of invisible barrier keeping the people in the pews and the pastors in the pulpit. It was weird.

Judging by the patterns I saw in church, the normal Christian life consisted of coming to Sunday services, contributing financially to support the church, being nice, and going home. "Committed" Christians might actually read the Bible on their own, pray for those in need, and if they were really into it, become part of a small group. "Fanatics" might occasionally invite their friends to church, but usually those friends wouldn't come. Church seemed nice enough, and I liked it, but there was one nagging thought that bothered me. This didn't look a lot like the life of Jesus or his followers I read about in the New Testament.

During my freshman year in college, God bumped me off a trajectory toward veterinary medicine and called me into a life of full-time vocational mission. Believe me, it wasn't my plan! However, it didn't take long for me to warm up to the idea. As I did, I came to understand the blueprints of the call God had given—introduce people to the saving grace of God and help them learn to follow Jesus so they can carry out his purpose in the world. Ten years later I graduated from seminary and was ordained a pastor with the benefit of education and training from some of the most respected institutions around the world. I was excited to get to work building the life and the church God had called me to lead. What I didn't know then was that I did not yet have the tools, the materials, or the practical knowledge to see the blueprints become a reality.

When I became an associate pastor, I simply did what I had seen those more experienced than me do—provide services and programs that would attract people to a church where they could encounter God, be changed, and then go change the world. Like my pastor before me, I wanted people to get more involved than just coming to Sunday services and going home. I wanted them to be transformed so they could be agents of transformation for others. Staff-organized and staff-led programs were the only tools I had been given. So I poured myself into designing and leading the best programs that would attract the most people to encounter God and be changed. And it seemed to be working! People started coming in greater numbers. Some lives were changed. But not many went out and changed the world.

The truth is as a young pastor I was already burning out, working crazy hours to provide these attractive services and programs. We desperately needed people to help us put on the many new programs we had designed and started. Plus there were all the other programs we had to keep going. Many of the people who came and participated in our services and programs loved what they got out of them. But no matter how much I preached on using your gifts to serve others, most simply came for what they could receive. Most were "too busy" to actually help put on our programs.

Those few who responded to my calls to serve ended up helping us run our many attractive programs. Very few of us though, myself included, were actually out in the world connecting with lost people the way that Jesus did. Even fewer of us were operating with the kind of spiritual power and authority Jesus exercised to transform lives. We talked about inviting our friends to church. Occasionally we organized a mission trip to go do good somewhere, but when we returned we still didn't spend much time or energy getting out and connecting with lost people in our neighborhoods, our schools, and our workplaces. We were simply too busy putting on our many quality programs at church!

Seven years into my ordained ministry, I had become a senior pastor and had the opportunity to organize and lead a whole congregation. We started diligently building programs that would help us attract people to our church so they could meet Jesus, follow him, and introduce him to others. Gradually we started seeing more people attending our programs. To accommodate them we had to build new buildings, hire more staff members, create new programs, and raise more money.

By most accounts our ministry was very successful. We had more people attending our programs than other churches of our denomination in our area. Our worship services became known as particularly effective because we put most of our time and resources into making them both attractive and impactful. We were put in a position to teach other leaders the methods we had developed. Books were published. Conferences were organized. It was affirming and exciting, but I still had a feeling something was wrong.

What was nagging at me in the midst of perceived success? It was that same feeling I had as a young leader, new to church—that what we were doing didn't look very much like the life of Jesus and his first followers. Even though we were preaching a lifestyle of discipleship to reach the world, our ministry revolved almost entirely around programs organized by our staff members, attended by the members of our church, and carried out on our church campus. After all, these were the only tools and raw materials we had been given. We were trying to build what the blueprint showed us, but we had inadequate tools, substandard materials, and no mentoring by those who knew how to do it. The problem wasn't with the blueprint—the problem was that we weren't producing what the blueprint described.

BUILDING A MOVEMENT

After twenty-five years I finally began to understand the problem. I had not yet learned to follow the pattern of life Jesus set for us to follow. Jesus never called his followers to attend church services and activities. He didn't command us to invite people to church or develop top-heavy, staff-led programs. Jesus never said the goal was to get more people attending programs. Instead he modeled a way of life for us and called us to follow that way by his grace. Through that way of life he trained, empowered, and sent his disciples out to bring the Good News of the Kingdom to lost and broken people where they lived. Jesus made disciples, formed a new kind of family, and in so doing built a Kingdom movement. He commissioned us to do the same.

My nagging sense of uneasiness in growing a "successful" church was the realization that we were doing none of those things effectively. We had become really good at producing spiritual consumers who liked attending the programs run by our staff and who were willing to support the church financially. The problem was that most of these people were "too busy" to get significantly involved in doing the things Jesus did in the world to seek and save the lost.

Jesus made it clear that fruit is what matters: *You did not choose me, but I chose you and appointed you so that you might go and bear fruit—fruit that will last* (John 15:16). He said some very sobering things about branches that don't bear this kind of lasting fruit. What is the kind of fruit that matters to Jesus? He showed us by example and commissioned us to follow him—to make the kind of disciples who produce more disciples who are empowered to carry out his mission together for the sake of the world. This is good fruit that lasts.

After eight years of trying to fulfill our mission by attracting people to church, things finally came to a head for me. I remember sitting in a difficult staff meeting with my dedicated team. For the umpteenth time we were discussing why, even after an entire year of focusing on God's call to use our gifts in serving others, we still weren't able to recruit the volunteers we needed to run our many programs. The strain on certain staff members had gotten so bad they shed tears while recounting their frustrations. I kept thinking, "What is wrong with this picture?"

Not long after that I went with the first team from our church to visit the hospital and orphan project we had gotten

After twenty-five years I finally began to understand the problem. I had not yet learned to follow the pattern of life Jesus set for us to follow. Jesus never called his followers to attend church services and activities. He didn't command us to invite people to church or develop top-heavy, staff-led programs. Jesus never said the goal was to get more people attending programs. Instead he modeled a way of life for us and called us to follow that way by his grace.

involved with in Uganda, East Africa. The organization we support had teamed up with a local church there to make a difference in a community with great needs. I watched my African brothers and sisters who had so little in the way of physical resources, giving literally everything they had in faith to see God's Kingdom come and his will be done. And it was working! They were providing clean water to the people of their community for the first time. They cared for over a thousand orphans with support from families in our church and others. People were walking a day's journey in order to receive medical and dental care. Men and women, young and old, were coming to faith by the hundreds, being discipled, and sent out to villages to multiply what God was doing in these places of need.

Every day I was with these loving people, I felt my own spiritual poverty more deeply. I had years of education and training, while their pastors had never even been to seminary, but they were bearing hundreds of times as much good fruit. I compared our fancy, multimedia worship center to their simple concrete structure, and yet they were reaching far more people and empowering them to reach others in ways we only dreamed of. Theirs was not a faith defined by programs or confined to a building. They demonstrated a way of life that looked a lot more like Jesus and the early church than any of the many churches in America I knew.

TIME FOR A CHANGE

I came home from my African epiphany realizing something had to change in me and in my church. God made it very clear to me that I was to seek after the love and spiritual power it takes to make disciples who can actually do what Jesus did in the world. Then and there I committed myself to answer the call—but I had no idea how to do it! We began to learn and teach biblical principles of living by God's power. The Holy Spirit started to become a more personal and practical part of our lives, and he produced more of the fruit of love and joy in our hearts. It was fun and even exciting, but I still did not see how this was going to empower us to reach the lost and see God's Kingdom transform the world.

About that time a good friend of mine told me about a church he had visited in Sheffield, England, called St. Thomas' Church. He told me this church in Northern England was different than any church we had seen in the U.S. He described a community of disciples who had learned how to make more disciples—a community of extended spiritual families who were living out the mission of God beyond the walls of their church. Although I had sworn off any more ministry conferences, my friend convinced me to visit St. Thomas', stay with a family from the church for ten days, and learn from them and their leaders.

I had been to bigger and more outwardly impressive churches in the US, but I had never visited a church like this. In a city where less than 2 percent of the population attended church, they were reaching more new people than they could accommodate in their buildings. In a culture where believing Christians are seen as a strange anomaly, they were connecting with their community outside the walls of the church and bringing the Good News to the places where lost people lived. In a context where nothing you could possibly do would attract people to church programs, they had learned how to be the church on mission in a way that was literally changing the face of their city.

Mike Breen was the leader of St. Thomas' for ten years, and with his team developed the vision, values, vocabulary, and vehicles that have been making a huge Kingdom impact ever since—not only on the city of Sheffield, but on cities, towns, and villages all around the world. As I listened to Mike teach that week, I started to understand what was different about this church: Discipleship. Not discipleship the way I had always understood and practiced it. Not discipleship as a class. Not discipleship that can be learned from a book. It was discipleship as a relationship. Discipleship as life-on-life mentoring. Discipleship as a way of life. The kind of discipleship that multiplies disciples who can in turn multiply disciples. The kind of discipling culture that empowers people to live out the mission of Jesus beyond the walls of the church.

At one of the teaching sessions, I was standing with Greg, our Teaching Pastor during a coffee break, and the janitor of the church came over and greeted us. I had seen him working around the church during that week. He was obviously a working-class man without a lot of formal education, yet he was very engaging. As we talked he asked what God had been saying to us through our time in Sheffield. We began to explain the new insights and hopes that were being stirred up by our experiences. He then asked what we thought God might want us to do about all that when we returned home. We described various ideas and possible plans for implementing what we were learning. As the break was coming to an end, he asked if he could pray for us, and we readily agreed.

Placing a hand on each of our shoulders, our new friend began to pray over us a powerful, Spirit-filled prayer inspiring faith in our hearts that we could learn to live out the things God was saying to us. When he finished the prayer, we thanked him, and he went back to his sweeping. As we returned to our seats for the next session, I turned to Greg and said, "That guy just ministered to us at a higher spiritual level than any of the leaders in our church is capable of!" This is the kind of fruit Jesus talked about; a community of disciples who are discipling others so everyone, from the pastors to the janitors, is equipped to carry out the mission of Jesus. I had always assumed it was my job to build a great church, and that doing so would produce disciples. That day Mike pointed out that Jesus said it works the other way around. Jesus said *"on this rock I will build the church"* (Matthew 16:18). He is telling us if we learn to make disciples who can make disciples, God will use them to build a great church.

As I spent more time in Sheffield, I began to understand this movement was not just about discipleship. It was about how discipleship empowers mission. I saw true discipleship was more about the way people were living out their lives with others than the programs they attended. I started to realize it was not primarily about what happened at church, but more about what was happening outside of the church buildings in their homes, schools, pubs, parks, and places of work. The people of St. Thomas' had learned how to build extended families of disciples who were living out the mission of Jesus in nearly every crack and crevice of a broken society.

Today there are literally hundreds of these Missional Communities spread out across Sheffield, a city of 1.5 million people. Some meet in upscale homes where they host wine and cheese parties to reach the upper classes. Some are comprised of people who have moved into the predominately immigrant neighborhoods where they are building friendships with Muslim families, showing them the Good News of Jesus. Others meet at 2 AM in a pub near the university to connect with college students who are far from God. Some are made up of people who like the outdoors and want to reach their friends who enjoy the same. Others are made up of youth who love soccer and want to share Jesus with their teammates. And on and on it goes.

Like the houseful of disciples that Jesus trained in the home of Peter and sent out on mission, these extended spiritual families are making disciples who are empowered to live the way Jesus lived. Like the early church that multiplied housefuls of disciples across the Mediterranean world in spite of every opposition, these families on mission are extending God's Kingdom against all odds. They are not just building a church or a minis-

> I had always assumed it was my job to build a great church, and that doing so would produce disciples. That day Mike pointed out that Jesus said it works the other way around. Jesus said "on this rock I will build the church" (Matthew 16:18). He is telling us if we learn to make disciples who can make disciples, God will use them to build a great church.

try at St. Thomas', but a Kingdom movement made up of families of disciples who are living out the mission of Jesus together as a Spirit-empowered way of life. And it is not just happening in Sheffield, but in places all over the world like Arhus, Zurich, Katmandu, Perth, Peru, Phoenix, and Fort Wayne.

AN INVITATION

I returned from Sheffield having made the decision that I wanted to spend the rest of my life learning how to build a church that could be a part of that kind of a Kingdom movement. I had found answers to many of my questions, but realized it was going to take years to implement what God had revealed to me in those ten days. Eight years later my personal walk with Jesus is profoundly different, and my understanding of how to carry out effective mission has undergone a fundamental shift. I assumed this journey was going to be about changing my church, but I discovered first and foremost it is about God changing me. It is about learning to do the things Jesus did the way Jesus did them. It is about my personal walk of faith, my marriage, my family, and the extended spiritual family on mission God is calling me to build. Then it is about the church I lead.

In nearly thirty years of marriage, nothing has strengthened my relationship with my wife the way learning to make disciples and live as a family on mission has. Although our sons are now adults, they and their loved ones are more a part of our lives than ever and are living out this discipling way of life with us. In our church we have seen the fruit of generations of disciples who can make disciples and live out the mission of Jesus in a way we never have before. This has deepened the spiritual maturity not only of our own church, but also the four new faith communities that have been planted by former leaders from our church in other places. It has not been without risks and sacrifice, but this new way of life is so rich we would never dream of going back to the way we used to live. The missional blueprint God gave me at the beginning of my call is still the same, but for the first time in my life I have been given the tools, materials, and the mentorship to actually build that kind of house.

If you want to define your Christian life by attending church services and programs, you are not going to like this book. If you simply want to get more people to come to your church, you will be disappointed as well. This book is written for all those who want to recover the life Jesus modeled for us and the movement into which he calls us. This book is written for those who want to build communities of people who are empowered to carry out the mission for which Jesus gave his life. It tells the story of my own journey, my family's journey, and that of my church. It tells the story of a movement that started in Sheffield, England and has spread around the world, equipping leaders, multiplying disciples, and releasing families on mission. It is a movement that is reclaiming the early church's way of life and combining it with practical tools for empowered missional discipleship in an intensely postmodern context. It offers an introduction to proven strategies and effective vehicles to meet these missional challenges and overcome.

Above all, this book is an invitation to stop trying to do it by yourself, and instead to become part of a relational movement of disciples who are learning how to restore the Church to her true calling. The call to make disciples and carry out the mission of Jesus by the power of his Spirit is simple, but way too hard to answer by yourself. You need others in your life who are seeking the same things and who are farther along in the journey. Good news: These people are out there. The Order of Mission is the relational network of leaders who share this vision and these values. The 3DM Network is the family of churches who share common vehicles, and vocabulary to carry out the mission of Jesus. 3DMovements is the training arm of this movement, dedicated to coaching and discipling leaders into the pattern Jesus set: making disciples who form the kind of communities which empower people to live out the mission of Jesus in the world.

Whether you are part of an established church, an innovative church, a house church, a megachurch, or a brand new church plant, I am personally inviting you to join us in learning this more abundant way of life. If you are willing to admit you need some mentors who can show you a better way to build that Kingdom future, then this invitation is for you. If you are tired of trying to drive nails with a screwdriver, and you long for the kind of tools that will empower you to see the blueprint of God's Kingdom become a reality, then read on and join us in learning what it looks like to empower missional disciples.

2

HOW DID WE END UP HERE?

FAIRY TALE OR OUR TALE?

Once upon a time, there was a feudal lord who owned all the land in the surrounding county. He had inherited the land from his father, who in turn had received it from his father. The lord lived in a huge stone manor set on a vast estate, and there he enjoyed the finest of everything society had to offer. Because agriculture and livestock were the primary sources of income, and these both required land in order to produce, the lord was very rich. If you owned the land, you owned the economy.

The only problem was the lord and his family did not like working the land that produced this income. They preferred relaxing in the comfort of their impressive stone manor, enjoying all their lovely things and the status they afforded. So the lords had worked out an arrangement with the common people, stretching back as many generations as anyone could remember. Later this arrangement would be called feudalism.

Under this social con-
tract, the feudal lord
provided land for the
people to grow food and
raise livestock. The lord
promised to provide all
those who worked his
lands protection from

bandits and other lords who might try to take their goods, as well as provision from the manor stockpiles for their families in times of famine. In
return the serfs, as they were called, vowed their fealty to the lord. This
means they agreed to pay back a portion of their income to the lord (sup-
porting his lavish lifestyle) and to fight in his army in case of war (protecting his wealth from other lords). The lord made sure the portion the serfs
were required to pay was high enough to prevent them from accumulating
wealth, thus keeping them dependent on him and ensuring the continuation of his comfort and control.

For a while this arrangement between the lord and his serfs functioned
smoothly—albeit more smoothly for the lord. The lord could measure his
income by the number of working serfs he had and the taxes they paid
him. The more tax-paying serfs he had, the greater his income, and therefore the greater his comfort, power, and prestige. The lord kept careful records of both his number of serfs and the taxes they paid. He liked quoting
these statistics to other lords who had fewer serfs and avoided the subject
with those lords who claimed more.

But one day war broke out between the lord's family and the family of a
neighboring lord. All the able-bodied male serfs were pressed into military
service and went out to fight the lord's battles. While they were gone, very
few crops were planted or harvested. The conflict raged on so long and
with such losses, that when it was over there were far fewer men to work
the fields. As a result income was greatly reduced, not only for the families
of the serfs, but also for the lord and his expensive manor.

A few years later, while the lord was try to recover from these losses, a prolonged famine hit. Drought killed most of the crops, and pestilence decimated the rest. It wasn't long before the hungry serfs came knocking at the door of the manor, asking the lord to provide for their families from his stockpiles of food and provisions. However, the lord had failed to build up adequate stockpiles. It had seemed unnecessary to him in times of peaceful prosperity. Besides, it was far more fun to spend the excess income on expanding the manor and filling it with art and luxury items. But you can't eat fine china or linen table clothes when the food runs out.

Faced with the realization that the lord was not fulfilling his end of the bargain, and realizing there was no food for their families, the serfs began to get restless. It became unclear what value there was to maintaining the traditional social contract. "Why should we continue to work the lord's land if there is no benefit to us and our families?" they asked themselves. As famine made the lord more vulnerable, the peasants grew increasingly rebellious. Inevitably, heads began to roll.

The former serfs demanded their independence and claimed portions of the lord's property for themselves. As individuals beholden to no lord, they could work their own land and keep all the income for themselves. Although the social protections were less, the opportunities for economic advancement were far greater. Few achieved the wealth and power the lord once enjoyed, but many increased their stake in the fruit of their labors. Over time this evolved into a free market society undergirded by the democratic system.

Strangely enough, in spite of these fundamental social shifts, the lord was not stripped of his title, nor was his manor house taken from him like the rest of his lands. It seemed the serfs had a nostalgic fondness for this relic from the past, so they allowed him to coexist with the new system, like a living museum exhibit. However, the lord soon discovered how expensive it was to maintain a fancy manor. Faced with extinction, the lord knew he had to adapt to these new realities. So he converted the serf's nostalgia for the manor into a viable business.

The lord began a marketing campaign, highlighting the treasures of the manor in order to attract visitors. He established an educational tour that introduced visitors to the splendors of the past and fostered an appreciation of their heritage. The business plan included various income streams in addition to the admission fees and tours, such as a chic coffee shop and a specialized gift store featuring every imaginable product emblazoned with the lord's crest. Although the lord was never able to match even a fraction of his previous wealth, he managed to survive and maintain the manor by working harder and harder to attract the attention of an ever more disinterested public. All the while he pined for the old days and wondered what had gone wrong.

BACK TO THE BEGINNING

Americans like me might find it difficult to identify with this tale, since it sounds so different from our own. Even casual students of history will recognize this story, while vastly oversimplified, is the story of medieval and modern Europe. Yet this story belongs also to Christian leaders in the developed western world. Whether we admit it, all church leaders in the west today sense that something is deeply amiss in our spiritual DNA. It is becoming increasingly clear that we have inherited a form of spiritual feudalism that has slowly been killing the church as we know it—even though it has more recently been propped up by desperate attempts at adaptation to the modern free-market system.

In case this seems like a confusing or unfounded statement to you, let's go a little bit further back in history and take a look at the beginning of our shared story. The Rabbi Jesus of Nazareth, who began his ministry in Galilee around 25 AD, seemed at first like many of his time. But soon it became clear that his was a life unlike any other. Jesus taught with unprecedented authority and healed with indisputable power. Soon large crowds gathered to hear his message of good news and to experience the freeing power of God's coming Kingdom that flowed through him.

From these crowds Jesus gathered together a smaller group of disciples who lived in the kind of relationship with him that not only taught them to know what he knew, but also to do what he did, and ultimately to become like him. Before long he trained them to go out on their own to find people who were open to them. He told them to stay with these people, eat with them, heal their sick, cast out demons, and tell them the Good News of the Kingdom.

While he trained these twelve disciples, he also shared life together with a larger houseful of disciples in the home of Peter and Andrew. They ate meals together, welcomed outsiders, and used this extended family as the base of their mission. After sending out the twelve on mission, Jesus then trained and sent out this houseful of seventy-two followers with his authority and power to find people who were open to them, and to do the very same things they had seen him do.

The temporal and religious authorities soon recognized the threat posed by this multiplication of authority and power. They moved quickly to protect their own status, attempting to squash the movement by cutting off its head. In human terms, the brutal execution of Jesus should have neutralized his followers through intimidation and lack of leadership. But it had the opposite effect. When his followers saw the crucified Jesus unmistakably alive again, they experienced a life-giving hope

It is becoming increasingly clear that we have inherited a form of spiritual feudalism that has slowly been killing the church as we know it—even though it has more recently been propped up by desperate attempts at adaptation to the modern free-market system.

that sustained them through the untold trials that were to come. Fifty days later they received the spiritual empowerment Jesus promised, which produced a quantum leap in their ability to do the things their Rabbi did.

From that day on, the followers of Jesus proclaimed a new Covenant of forgiveness in Jesus and demonstrated the power of God's Kingdom to give people a new kind of life, fulfilling Jesus' prediction that they would do even greater things than he did. Large crowds gathered in Jerusalem, attracted by the liberating power of God that was released through them. The movement Jesus began continued to grow by multiplication rather than addition, because its leaders followed Jesus' example of training smaller groups of disciples who could do what they did, with exponential results. These rapidly multiplying disciples gathered in homes as extended spiritual families (Greek: *oikos*), and these households provided the support needed to continue extending the mission of Jesus in spite of the great pressure brought to bear against them.

Like those first authorities in Jerusalem who tried to stamp out the Jesus movement at its inception, Roman officials all over the Empire desperately tried to halt its rapid expansion through increasingly brutal and public intimidation—but to no avail. Because the basic DNA of Jesus was replicated in each disciple through the process of multiplication, more of his followers were always ready to take the place of those who were executed or banished. Because they lived as part of an extended family that shared a common mission, they could continue to carry out their commission even in the face of constant opposition. Because they claimed the authority Jesus had given them and yielded to a power greater than themselves, they were able to overcome otherwise impossible obstacles.

Rodney Stark, in his seminal study The Rise of Christianity, demonstrates conclusively that over 50 percent of the entire Roman Empire had embraced the Christian faith by the time of Constantine the Great. The subtitle of his book captures the enormity of this historical anomaly: *How the*

Obscure, Marginal Jesus Movement Became the Dominant Religious Force in the Western World in a Few Centuries.[1] Looking at the simple historical facts, we begin to realize the spiritual potency of the early church was qualitatively different than that of the church in the developed western world today.

WHAT WENT WRONG?

What happened to this contagious viral movement that challenged and overcame the greatest authorities and powers of its day? Why do churches in the places where this movement first took root now stand largely empty and lifeless? Why is Christianity seen as irrelevant and out of place in the western centers of culture and power today?

We like to describe the root cause of this spiritual impotence as spiritual feudalism. It began when a Roman mandate, entitled The Edict of Milan, ultimately neutered this seemingly unstoppable force for personal and social transformation launched by Jesus and his followers less than three centuries earlier.

In summer of the year AD 313, Emperor Constantine, who ruled the western parts of the Roman Empire, and his counterpart Licinius, who ruled the East, were in Milan to celebrate the wedding of Constantine's sister with Licinius. As consummate politicians they realized the movement Jesus had begun was winning the day, and so

1.   Rodney Stark, The Rise of Christianity (Princeton: Princeton University Press, 1996)

they decided it was time co-opt this power for their own ends. The advice of a modern pragmatist comes to mind: "If you can't beat 'em, join 'em!" The Edict they issued proclaimed freedom of worship for Christians so that "any Divinity whatsoever in the seat of the heavens may be propitious and kindly disposed to us and all who are placed under our rule."[2] They were simply covering their bases.

Constantine effectively managed to pour the dynamic, transforming movement of Jesus into the mold of Roman patronage, and the result was the institutional forms of church which have endured until our day. Roman society at that time was based on a system of mutually beneficial obligatory relationships. The *senatorial* class was comprised of those who wielded the highest levels of political and military power. They owned the vast majority of arable land and were dominated by Caesar himself and his imperial household. The *equestrian* class was made up of successful business owners, mostly Roman citizens, whose base was a household of relatives, slaves, and business associates. By far the largest segment of the population was comprised of the *commoner* and *slave* classes, tied to the nobility by working their lands and fighting in their armies. These lower classes enjoyed the protection and provision of the nobility by giving up power and allowing their patrons to rule over them.

Each of these three classes was bound by obligation to those higher on the social ladder. Patrons offered employment, legal representation, and other social benefits to those below them in return for their clients' political, military, and social support. This patronage was not only an economic arrangement, but also an important social system. Clients gathered in the

---

2.   From Lactantius, De Mort. Pers., ch. 48. opera, ed. 0. F. Fritzsche, II, p. 288 sq. (Bibl Patr. Ecc. Lat. XI). Translated in University of Pennsylvania. Dept. of History: Translations and Reprints from the Original Sources of European History (Philadelphia: University of Pennsylvania Press (1897, 1907), Vol 4:1, p. 28-30. This text is in the public domain.

atrium and vestibule of their patron's estate for the morning *salutation*, an opportunity to be received by their patron and receive the benefits of their social power. In return the clients were expected to accompany their patron to the Roman forum in a noisy show of public support. The clients and the patrons wore carefully differentiated clothing to highlight the disparity in their social class.

CO-OPTING A MOVEMENT

Jesus went to great lengths to ensure he could share a final Passover dinner with his closest disciples. At that symbolic meal he prophetically warned his disciples not to be co-opted by the patron-client culture of Rome when he said, *"The kings of the Gentiles exercise lordship over them, and those in authority over them are called benefactors. But not so with you. Rather, let he greatest among you become as the youngest, and the leader as one who serves."* (Luke 22:25-26)

The benefactor style of leadership is one in which power and provision are doled out to those who need it in order to maintain a position of superiority and control. Jesus explicitly told the leaders of his movement this is not the way they were to operate. Through his example, Jesus showed them that leaders in his movement are to raise up others to lead and lay down their lives in order to accomplish that. For nearly three hundred years, this discipling style of leadership fueled a transforming movement no king or emperor could stop, because there was a constant supply of new, trained and equipped leaders to rise up and take the place of those who were imprisoned or martyred. Sadly, this empowering leadership culture was ultimately subsumed by Roman hegemony.

> Constantine effectively managed to pour the dynamic, transforming movement of Jesus into the mold of Roman patronage, and the result was the institutional forms of church which have endured until our day.

As the Christian movement was folded into Roman society after AD 313, the church began to reflect the shape of its surrounding culture, rather than the other way around. Almost imperceptibly the clergy began to adopt a posture of patronage toward the laity, taking on the responsibility for spiritual leadership and oversight, while expecting from their clientele obligatory obedience, financial support, and attendance at public services. Soon bishops adopted dress differentiating them from ordinary priests, who in turn wore clothing which set them apart from the common people. These religious patrons expected their clients to make a public show of support by joining them as they paraded their status in grand religious basilicas that rivaled even the senatorial halls of the Roman forum.

Even though Paul had made it clear three hundred years earlier that "there is no longer Jew or Greek, there is no longer slave or free, there is no longer male and female; for all of you are one in Christ Jesus" (Galatians 3:28), the newly legalized church embraced the hierarchy of Roman social norms, and the Bible became the sole domain of the clerical elite. Although Luke records the fulfillment on Pentecost of God's promise through Joel that he would pour out his Spirit upon all flesh, spiritual authority and power eventually became the exclusive right of the religious upper class. In spite of Jesus' clear call for all to follow his example, it wasn't long before the involvement of ordinary people in discipleship and mission, which had characterized the explosive origins and early growth of the Christian movement, began to disappear completely.

> The benefactor style of leadership is one in which power and provision are doled out to those who need it in order to maintain a position of superiority and control. Jesus explicitly told the leaders of his movement this is not the way they were to operate.

Now the die was cast that would shape the forms of Christianity for the coming millennium. Roman patronage came to define the roles of clergy and laity in the church. A kind of spiritual amnesia regarding the pattern of life set by Jesus and his first followers was institutionalized. Somewhere along the way, following Jesus and living as an extended family on mission together was replaced by church attendance and sacramental observance. Followers of the Way, the Truth, and the Life were co-opted by the ways of this world rather than the Kingdom Jesus established.

But there was a still deeper kind of amnesia yet to come.

3

FROM PATRONAGE TO CONSUMERISM

FROM CLIENT TO CONSUMER

As the Roman Empire faded into the background and medieval Europe took its place, similar social structures evolved and shaped the forms of the church. The land-owning Roman nobility became feudal lords. The commoners and slaves became their indentured serfs. The church continued to conform to the shape of society. Bishops received the title *Lord*, took up residence in their *palaces*, and assumed power to appoint parish priests called *patronage*. Tithes were considered obligatory taxes paid by the ordinary people to their clerical lords. Members of the laity were expected to attend the services led by their spiritual patrons in return for the promised protection from spiritual famine and eternal damnation. More than ever spiritual authority and power were institutionalized in these ecclesiastical structures, while discipleship and mission, if acknowledged at all, were relegated to the professional clergy.

We can see these dynamics at work today in all the denominations that trace their historical roots back to European soil and even the far reaches of the Roman Empire, including those benefiting from the insights of the Reformation and subsequent renewal movements in the Old World. Luther sensed how wrong things had gone in Rome and understood the key to reformation was putting the Bible back into the hands of the people. In doing so, he began a revolution that is still being played out in the lives of all those who actually open its now readily available pages and read. However, the revolution was subverted again by the generations immediately following Luther.

Luther took the Bible out of the hands of popes and priests and put it into the hands of ordinary people. But the Scholastics who followed Luther put the Bible firmly back into the hands of the pastors and professors, well beyond the reach of those for whom it was intended. The inheritors of this spiritual hierarchy include Anglicans, Lutherans, Presbyterians, Mennonites, Methodists, and Baptists. Even today most members of protestant churches feel the Bible is beyond them and instead look to their pastors to feed them spiritually, based on the biblical training they received from their professors. In this we see the continuation of the patron-client relationship, a kind of spiritual feudalism that stretches back some 1700 years.

One test of this is to ask what we count in our churches. If we are honest we will have to admit that, like the feudal lords who counted numbers of serfs and taxes, the two key metrics for most churches today are attendance and tithes. In the end, the Reformation was the right first step, but it didn't go far enough. Luther, Calvin, and their contemporaries restored us to the new Covenant of grace in Jesus' death and resurrection, but fell short of reintroducing us to the power of living as part of God's coming Kingdom where we all multiply disciples who carry out the mission of Jesus.

About the time Luther and various Reformers introduced Europe to the Bible, Columbus and other explorers introduced the New World to the

Old. The colonization of North America provided new soil in which the children of the reformation could plant their physical and spiritual seeds. Unfettered from the feudal system of their homeland, these pioneers began to establish a new cultural system valuing individual responsibility and initiative over status and privilege. Informed by thinkers like John Locke and Adam Smith, they began the great experiment of a democratic nation based on a free market economy.

> Luther took the Bible out of the hands of popes and priests and put it into the hands of ordinary people. But the Scholastics who followed Luther put the Bible firmly back into the hands of the pastors and professors, well beyond the reach of those for whom it was intended.

This New World not only provided greater opportunities for geographical, political, and economic exploration, but also provided the chance for spiritual innovation as well. This is why the renewal movement begun by John Wesley in England took root in America in a way it never could have in Wesley's homeland. Multiple waves of holiness revivals, from the so-called "Burned-Over District" in upstate New York to a tiny church on Azusa Street in Los Angeles, give testimony to the entrepreneurial climate of this new world. These kinds of innovative movements in America over the past century have given rise to newer networks like the Assemblies of God, the Foursquare Church, Calvary Chapel, and the Vineyard, attesting to the continuation of this pioneering spirit.

In spite of this fertile new soil, churches transplanted from Europe carried with them much of their Old World feudal DNA. Though Protestant bishops and clergy in America may not enjoy all the temporal benefits provided by the European state church systems, they can still operate in the same kind of ecclesiastical feudalism that keeps ordinary Christians functioning like religious serfs.

The churches that sprang from American soil have avoided certain aspects of the feudal model, but unfortunately many have been co-opted by another system. Whereas Constantine poured the early Christian movement into the mold of Roman patronage, many American churches have been profoundly shaped by the mold of democratic capitalism. Ours is a free market system where church shopping makes complete sense to most people because the focus is on meeting the perceived needs of an individual. Over the past fifty years, churches in America have continued this pattern by placing an ever-greater emphasis on attracting new members by providing staff-led programs tailored to the specific interests of various constituencies.

The steady decline of participation in American church life in since 1960 is a pale reflection of the massive migration out of the church that has taken place in postmodern Europe during that same period. The feudal system of European churches has become so irrelevant in its largely secular culture that many there question the future viability of the church at all. American church attendance, on the other hand, has benefited from the delayed encroachment of postmodernity, and yet growing secularism has pressured churches in the new world to focus greater attention on meeting the perceived needs of members and prospective recruits. In the middle of the last century American churches began offering specialized programs targeted at the heart of the family: children's and youth ministry. Eventually they began hiring specially trained staff members to provide professional quality programming for literally every stage of life.

The seeker-targeted churches of the last few decades took this free-market approach to a new level as they began to aggressively market their services and programs to those who had little or no background or interest in the Christian faith or church. This became the stated purpose of the primary weekly worship gatherings in these ministries. Eventually, many mainline and even European churches sought to implement this kind of client-driven methodology to reverse their catastrophic decline in church participation and faith. Even now most church planting strategies focus on how to attract new people to the various services they can provide. The churches in America that were able to attract large numbers of people to participate in their services and programs gave hope that this approach was the silver bullet needed to renew the Christian movement at the end of the twentieth century. But aside from a handful of celebrity-level exceptions, this is proving to be a short-lived hope.

With about 4 percent of the Millennial generation in America currently attending church services on a regular basis, and every other demographic category declining significantly as well, it is clear this attractional model is falling woefully short. Megachurches absorbing transfers from smaller churches less able to meet the consumer demand does not constitute a reversal of the trend. Apparently we need more than a better marketing plan or a new program to solve this crisis.

What began as a dynamic grass-roots movement in Palestine that nearly conquered the Roman Empire gradually became a theology in Greece, an institution in Rome, a state church in Europe, and a non-profit service-provider in America.

The question is: what will be the next chapter of our story?

BEYOND FEUDALISM AND CONSUMERISM

On a recent trip to England, my wife Pam and I spent a day touring the massive estate of the Duke and Duchess of Devonshire called Chatsworth House. Built in 1549 by Sir William Cavendish, the thirty breathtaking rooms of this three-story manor are lavishly adorned with sculpted marble, fitted with countless gilt-carvings, and stuffed with classical art. Sur-

rounded by a thousand acres of fantastically sculpted gardens and five miles of walking paths, a day is hardly enough to take in the spectacle of this monument to the feudal upper class.

After seven straight hours of marveling at the lavish lifestyle that produced such a place, we could not ignore the irony when the tour ended in a typical tourist gift shop, filled with postcards, t-shirts, beach towels, and mugs, each bearing the crest of the esteemed Cavendish family. I felt like I was exiting a ride at Disneyland! Combined with the steep admission price and various options for audio tours and added attractions, this naked display of capitalism in a shrine to aristocratic privilege made me laugh out loud.

It is natural for the Duke and Duchess to employ the business strategies of a free-market economy to keep their lavish estate operating, because the days of feudalism are long gone. This is the only way such a relic from the past can be preserved, and even that may not be enough to keep pace with the steady decay of such an unwieldy monument. The day may well come when the Chatsworth House has to be converted into swanky condos if public fascination with the luxuries of the past begins to wane.

This is exactly the predicament that my church and many like it face today. We have inherited a long-extinct feudal system in which the established members function much like religious serfs, offering their attendance and tithes, while clergy like me are expected to offer spiritual provision and protection. But, like the Cavendish family, we find ourselves living in a time when feudalism no longer operates, and a free-market economy rules the day. As a result, we search endlessly for ways to market ourselves to a population that sees us as a quaint throwback from an irrelevant past. What a far cry from those first followers of Jesus who converted and transformed a violent pagan empire!

The churches and leaders that sprang from American soil and managed to avoid inheriting a primarily feudal culture are faced with a separate though similar predicament. These newer expressions of Christianity are thoroughly steeped in the free-market economy and reflect a more indigenous culture than their European-transplant cousins. By proclaiming the message of Jesus in an individualistic framework with a pioneering spirit, these newer churches were able to establish themselves and made significant inroads in the second half of the last century. At one time simply worshiping in non-religious buildings with rock bands and casually dressed preachers who proclaimed a clearly applicable and empowering message was enough to attract increasing numbers of attendees. But not anymore.

Growing postmodern skepticism and resistance to any kind of organized religion are beginning to overtake the gains of culturally relevant expressions of Christian faith as well. A deeper cultural shift is taking place that is leading us toward a thoroughly secular and ultimately pagan society. Our brothers and sisters in Europe and Australasia can well attest to that fact. Alan Hirsch, a missional veteran schooled in the postmodern streets of Melbourne, tells us the time has come for a "holy rebellion" among the institutional forms of church that have taken us so far from the organic movement Jesus began. He says, "The change of thinking needed in our day as far as the church and its mission are concerned must be radical indeed; that is, it must go to the roots of the problem... We simply have to find a way to push past the historical answers that so easily suggest themselves to people whose imagination of what it means to be God's people has been taken hostage to a less than biblical imagination of church."[3]

The Christian movement has come to a crucial crossroads; what the New Testament calls a *kairos*. At a *kairos* crossroads, you have the opportunity to choose a new path. We must come to terms with the fact that much of our current way of doing church is not rooted in the pattern set for us by Jesus

---

3.   Alan Hirsch, *The Forgotten Ways: Reactivating the Missional Church* (Grand Rapids: Brazos, 2006), Section One, part 1, phase three.

and his first followers. This is the core problem threatening the viability of the church today. Neil Cole, organic church planter and pioneer, received a vision of a zombie-like bride with pale green saggy skin and disintegrating bridal gown, weakly lying back on a couch with a sickly smile on her face. He knew immediately God was giving him a picture of the ailing American church today, assuming all is well, but producing so little good fruit. Cole writes, "Apparently, the world is interested in Jesus; it is his wife that they do not want to spend time with."[4]

Many people who are fascinated with Jesus are no longer willing to engage with the Bride of Christ because we have strayed so far from the life Jesus modeled for us. The time has passed where we can fall back on simply trying to make our current ecclesial forms more culturally relevant. There is no hipper, cooler, or more tech-saavy way of reaching the newer generations—or their parents for that matter. Nor is going old school and reverting to comfortable or curious traditions the answer. We are not going to market or incentivize our way out of this dilema. The only answer is radical-we must go back to the beginning of our story to recover the roots of Jesus' movement.

Every student of postmodernity knows that in many ways the 21st century is more like the first century than the twentieth century was. Will this next era of church history be looked back on as another dark ages for the church or an era of Christian reformation and renaissance? It all depends on how we respond to the challenge. Will we cling to a long-lost feudal system by focusing on the number of our members and the amounts of their tithes? Will we be co-opted by a consumer culture through one more marketing campaign or the latest relevant program to boost attendance and offerings? Or will we reclaim the three key elements of the movement Jesus began: living in the authority and power Jesus passed on to his followers, multi-

---

4.   Neil Cole, *Organic Church: Growing Faith Where Life Happens* (San Francisco: Jossey-Bass, 2005), p. xxii.

plying disciples as Jesus did, and learning to live by that power as families on mission?

Jesus' call is simple and clear: "Come, follow me, and I will send you out to fish for people." (Mark 1:17) If we are willing to go back and relearn how to follow the pattern Jesus set for us, we will discover what it means to be part of that powerful movement by which God is redeeming the whole world.

> We are not going to market or incentivize our way out of this dilema. The only answer is radical-we must go back to the beginning of our story to recover the roots of Jesus' movement.

4

JESUS' THREE-DIMENSIONAL LIFE

LIVING IN FLATLAND

Imagine life without dimension. It is hard because we only know a dimensional world, but try. Life without dimension means you can't move up or down. You can't move to the left or to the right. You can't go forward or backward. You can only be where you are. A non-dimensional world is literally a single point. Like a mathematical point, it has no area and takes up no space. It is smaller than the head of a pin. It can't contain anything. It is simply a single point. Period.

Now let's move into one dimension. You can't move up or down. You can't move to the left or to the right. You can only go forward or backward. Your world is a line. It is an infinitely narrow line. Like the one-dimensional point, it has no width whatsoever—it is thinner than the thinnest sheet of paper. This thin line simply goes on forever in each direction.

When we add another dimension, our line becomes a plane. In this two-dimensional world you can move forward and backward. You can move to the left and to the right. In fact, you can move in every horizontal direction. But there is no moving up or down, not even a little bit. Again, this plane is immeasurably thin. It has no vertical dimension at all.

In this two-dimensional world only flat shapes are possible. Lines can become triangles, squares, pentagons, all kinds of polygons, even circles. For those who inhabit a two-dimensional world, these shapes are almost indistinguishable, because you can only see the edge of things. In our three-dimensional world we would simply lift our heads above the horizon in order to look down on the shapes. But in a two-dimensional world, it is impossible to look down on anything, because there is no up or down.

If a three-dimensional object or being entered into a two-dimensional world, it would appear as a flat shape because only a slice of its form would fit into this plane. For instance, a sphere would appear as a circle, and a cube would appear as a square. Imagine how difficult it would be for the inhabitants of a two-dimensional world to comprehend a three-dimensional visitor. They would only see an infinitely thin slice of that visitor— and even that would be visible only from its razor edge.

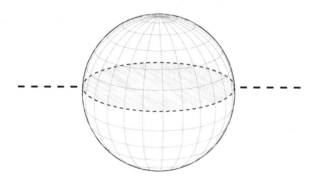

In 1884 an English clergyman and schoolmaster named Edwin A. Abbott wrote a ground-breaking satirical novella entitled *Flatland: A Romance of Many Dimensions.*[5] With great attention to detail, he described the world called "Flatland," a two-dimensional world inhabited by lines and shapes living in a class conscious-society based on a kind of feudal system. One day a Sphere is sent from the three-dimensional world called Spaceland to try and convince the

citizens of Flatland that a third dimension exists beyond their experience.

The Sphere visits a particular Square, to whom he patiently explains and then demonstrates the mind-blowing realities of a three-dimensional world. Seeing how hard it is for the Square to comprehend such foreign concepts, the Sphere develops carefully constructed analogies to help him understand. These help, but ultimately fall short. In addition the Sphere uses his own unique attributes to demonstrate three-dimensionality, but the Square dismisses these as magic tricks. Finally, the only way the Sphere can convince the Square that a third dimension actually exists is to lead him into that dimension so he can experience it for himself. Once the Square experiences this new reality, he finally begins to get it and ultimately accepts a call to evangelize Flatland with the Gospel of Three Dimensions. This task is far more difficult than he anticipates—his message is received with hostility and persecution. The Square finally lands in prison for his claims about the Third Dimension.

---

5. Edwin A. Abbott, *Flatland: A Romance in Many Dimensions* (United Kingdom: Seely & Co., 1884).

JESUS IN FLATLAND

Abbot's Flatland has been hailed for more than a century as a masterpiece on many levels: socially, politically, and mathematically. When I first read it, the theological message is what stood out head and shoulders above the rest. When Jesus appeared in Galilee proclaiming the Good New's of God's coming Kingdom, he was describing a new dimension to our reality no less revolutionary than trying to describe Spaceland to the residents of Flatland. Knowing this new reality would be nearly impossible to understand and receive simply as an abstract concept, Jesus not only talked about it, but demonstrated it in his own life and in the impact he made on others.

The more I learn to base my life on the specific patterns Jesus modeled for us, the clearer it becomes that Jesus lived, and invites us to live, a three-dimensional kind of life. One day in the life of Jesus is sufficient to illustrate these three dimensions. When Jesus decided to form his core group of disciples, he withdrew to a remote mountainside where he *"spent the night praying to God"* (Luke 6:12). This is a vivid description of what was for Jesus the primary dimension of his life; his relationship with the Father. This dimension was so central and profound that Jesus described it this way: *"Very truly I tell you, the Son can do nothing by himself; he can do only what he sees his Father doing, because whatever the Father does the Son also does. For the Father loves the Son and shows him all he does."* (John 5:19-20)

After he spent that night in prayer, Jesus carefully chose twelve disciples in whom to invest his life (Luke 6:13-16). Discipleship in first-century Palestine was a deeply committed, covenantal relationship in which the Rabbi invited his disciples to share every aspect of his life so they could become like him. For the rest of his ministry on earth, Jesus lived in the closest kind of community with these twelve disciples and a wider circle of disciples whom he called friends. Jesus could have decided to proclaim his message as a solitary sage and preacher, but instead he intentionally chose to live in close relational community with others.

This is the second key dimension of Jesus' life, the nature of which he expressed on the last night he was with his disciples. After washing their feet and sharing a sacred meal, he said, *"A new command I give you: Love one another. As I have loved you, so you must love one another. By this everyone will know that you are my disciples, if you love one another."* (John 13:34-35)

That same morning, Jesus came down from the mountainside with his twelve disciples, joined up with a larger group of his followers, and gathered a large crowd of people from all over Israel and the wider region of Palestine. He proclaimed the Good News of the new Covenant God was making with his people and the powerful Kingdom that was being unleashed. Jesus not only described this Covenant and Kingdom with words, but he also demonstrated it by his actions. As Jesus claimed the authority given to him by the Father, divine power flowed through him to heal the broken and release those in spiritual captivity (Luke 6:17-19). Jesus didn't limit himself to only two dimensions: a relationship with God and the supportive relationships of community. He also lived in this third dimension of reaching out with God's love and power to those in the wider world.

This powerful third relational dimension, flowing out of the depth of the other two, is what made Jesus' life truly revolutionary. The very idea of building relationships with such outsiders was controversial among the religious leaders of his day. When Jesus invited the tax collector Levi into his life and had dinner at Levi's home, the Pharisees and teachers of the law complained to his disciples, *"Why do you eat and drink with tax collectors and sinners?' Jesus answered them, 'Those who are well have no need of a physician, but those who are sick. I have not come to call the righteous but sinners to repentance.'"* (Luke 5:30-32) Jesus' opponents vehemently tried to deny the powerful impact he had on these outsiders was real, even seeking to discredit Jesus' power as

> When Jesus appeared in Galilee proclaiming the Good News of God's coming Kingdom, he was describing a new dimension to our reality no less revolutionary than trying to describe Spaceland to the residents of Flatland.

evil (Luke 11:15). But the fruit of Jesus' life was undeniable. The power that flowed through him was obviously good and from God because it consistently produced healing, wholeness, reconciliation, and liberation.

UP   with the Father

IN   with the disciples

OUT   with the world[6]

We have come to understand these three key dimensions of Jesus' life as the basic pattern he has set for our lives as his followers. We have learned to express this pattern to those we lead using the simple shape of a triangle, each point representing one of these three dimensions:

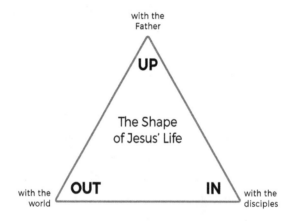

The first time someone showed me this powerful tool, I thought it was kind of gimmicky, maybe because it was so simple. Once I began to engage in intentional discipleship, I quickly realized the value of a visual symbol that conveys a key principle from Jesus' life and that can be easily remembered and passed on.

---

6.   Mike Breen, *Building a Discipling Culture* (Pawley's Island: 3DM Publishing, 2009), p. 67-83.

Like the other LifeShapes I will introduce in this book, the Triangle is simply a transferable biblical tool designed to help us follow Jesus and train other disciples to make disciples as well. If we are going to become the kind of disciples who can multiply disciples who do the same, we will need a toolbox full of these practical, biblical tools that we can pass on to others. The Triangle is the first tool in that toolbox. It is a pattern to help us gauge our growth as we become more like Jesus in these three key aspects of our lives. It operates like a picture because it shows us the shape of Jesus' life, like a mirror because it shows us where we are not like Jesus, and like a window because it gives us a vision of who we are becoming in God's Kingdom.

When I first visited St. Thomas' Church in Sheffield, my friend Greg Wallace and I stayed with the McCabes, a lovely family from the church. About the second day we were with them, the husband Pete explained why he was going to visit the soup kitchen that Saturday morning: "I think my UP is pretty healthy and my IN is going well, but I sense God has been calling me to invest in my OUT lately. So I am going to see if this might be a place where I can grow in my care for those outside the church." At the time I still didn't fully understand the language he was using, but it was clear that here was a man who had received a tool that was helping him learn how to live more like Jesus did.

Like the Sphere demonstrating three-dimensional life to the residents of Flatland, the three-dimensional shape of Jesus' life shows us what it is like to live in God's Kingdom where his will can be done on earth as it is in heaven. Picture the cramped confines of living in Flatland, and then imagine the wonder of stepping into the expansive realm of Spaceland. In this three-dimensional Kingdom that Jesus brings, our capacity for living the life we were designed to live dramatically increases. That is what Jesus means when he says to those who will follow his voice, *"I have come that they may have life, and have it abundantly"* (John 10:10). This abundant life is not necessarily filled with more possessions or pleasures, as Jesus and his early followers demonstrate, but it is a life with greater capacity for what Jesus called *"complete joy"* (John 15:11). In this three-dimensional Kingdom, not only does our cup overflow, but the capacity of our cup grows as well!

IN FLATLAND TODAY

Think back to our earlier comparison of the world-changing movement of early Christianity with the patron/client institutionalization of the later church. What made the first three hundred years of the Jesus' movement so revolutionary is that the three dimensions of Jesus' life were continually multiplied in the lives of others. People were saved by God's grace through faith in Jesus, and they were also mentored into these three relational dynamics Jesus modeled for us. Their corporate life together was shaped by Jesus' three-dimensional way of life. The more clearly we come to understand these three dimensions of Jesus' life, the more clearly we will see how to recover the transformational power of the early Christian movement in our lives, our families, and our churches today.

The crisis we are facing in the 21st century is that too many of us are still living in Flatland. Many of us who claim to be followers of Jesus do not actually do the things he did. We focus on the Good News that we have been saved through Jesus' sacrifice on the cross, but we often don't learn how to live out the full implications of that salvation in our daily lives.

> Like the Sphere demonstrating three-dimensional life to the residents of Flatland, the three-dimensional shape of Jesus' life shows us what it is like to live in God's Kingdom where his will can be done on earth as it is in heaven.

Many communities of those who claim Jesus' name do not reflect the shape of his life. When you look honestly at your own life, do you see all three dimensions of Jesus' life represented in the same proportion as his? Are you actively seeking to grow in the dimensions of Jesus' life that are lacking in yours? Lots of Christians today are living two-dimensional, Flatland kinds of lives, and are missing out on the abundant, fruitful life Jesus promised.

Some of us are focused on our relationship with God (UP) and with other believers (IN), but don't invest significantly in building relationships with those who are not yet part of the family of God (OUT). Others of us are passionate about God (UP) and seeking the lost (OUT), but we are trying to do it on our own and are missing out on the strength of community (IN). Still others are invested in the church (IN) and serving those outside the church (OUT), but are trying to do it on their own strength rather than learning to operate in the authority and power of God (UP).

Jesus has come into our flattened out world to show us a better world. His three-dimensional life is the fruitful life we were created to live. Jesus is calling us to follow him into this new world where we can learn to live a more abundant, Jesus-shaped life and help others learn to do the same.

5

EXPLORING SPACELAND

THE SPACES IN JESUS' CHURCH

Wouldn't you like to be a member of Jesus' church? Literally. Locally. What would your church look like if Jesus was the pastor? To answer this question, we need look no further than the kind of community Jesus formed. Just as Jesus' life shaped the lives of individuals who followed him, so it shaped their life together as well. Wherever Jesus went he built community in three particular ways—UP with the Father, IN with the disciples, and OUT with the world. This forms the essential pattern for our life together if we want to truly live as a community of his followers.

Sociologists have long understood that human beings instinctively gather together in four different sized groups that function in four distinct ways.

In 1966 Edward T. Hall introduced the concept of Proxemics, observing how people interact differently in four distinct settings:[7]

PUBLIC SPACE   These are large groups of hundreds or thousands of people who gather around a common sense of identity, often to hear a public speaker or witness an event. Think of tens of thousands of football fans jammed into a stadium or fellow Apple devotees tuning in to a live webcast of the latest product launch. This is a tribe.

SOCIAL SPACE   These are mid-sized groups of 20-50 people who know each other and share common values or purpose. Think of a big family reunion or a houseful of people at your annual Christmas party. This is an extended family.

PERSONAL SPACE   These are smaller groups of 4-12 people who have a strong sense of relational connection and share a significant portion of their lives together. Think of your immediate family or a group of roommates. This is a nuclear family.

INTIMATE SPACE   These are groupings of two or three people who are deeply committed to each other and share everything. Think of a romantic relationship or close friendships. This is a marriage or best friends.

7.   Edward T. Hall, *The Hidden Dimension* (New York: Anchor Books, 1966).

Hall's study demonstrated that healthy community consists of people who live in all four spaces and gain a sense of belonging in each. Nearly fifty years after this groundbreaking research, Joseph Myers applied Hall's observations to the way we build a sense of belonging in Christian communities, demonstrating that large worship gatherings and small groups alone are not enough for healthy Christian community. Myers says it this way: "All belonging is significant. Healthy community—the goal humankind has sought since the beginning—is achieved when we hold harmonious connections within all four spaces."[8]

What neither Hall nor Myers might have realized is Jesus formed community in exactly this way. Even a cursory look at the Gospels reveals the pattern Jesus followed in gathering people together:

> Jesus gathered people into **Public Space**: *"a large crowd was gathering and people were coming to Jesus from town after town"* (Luke 8:4).

> Jesus gathered people into **Social Space**: *"After this the Lord appointed seventy-two others and sent them, two by two, ahead of him to every town and place where he was about to go."* (Luke 10:1)

> Jesus gathered people into **Personal Space**: *"When morning came, he called his disciples to him and chose twelve of them, whom he also designated apostles"* (Luke 6:13).

> Jesus gathered people into **Intimate Space**: *"About eight days after Jesus said this, he took Peter, John and James with him and went up onto a mountain to pray."* (Luke 9:28)

---

8. Joseph R. Myers, *The Search to Belong* (Grand Rapids: Zondervan, 2003), p. 51.

Jesus built the foundations for healthy and fruitful community by modeling the way life is meant to be lived in all four communal spaces. Not surprisingly, these differing spaces corresponded to the three primary dimensions of Jesus' life.

When Jesus gathered *large crowds* together he was modeling all three dimensions of Kingdom life, but the dimension that people experienced the most powerfully was the UP dimension. They heard God's authority in the teaching of Jesus. They saw God's power released through his miraculous healings and people being freed from demonic possession. Jesus demonstrated to us that, while all three dimensions of his life operate in Public Space, these large gatherings are most effective at helping people grow in the UP dimension.

When Jesus gathered a *smaller group* of twelve disciples, again all three dimensions were functioning, but the IN dimension was the most significant. They shared their lives together and built close relationships with each other. Out of this deep connection and trust, Jesus was able to offer them the significant challenges that would form them into disciples who could do what he did. Jesus shows us that Personal Space is best suited to develop the IN dimension of our lives.

When Jesus gathered his followers into a *mid-sized group*, he specifically focused on the OUT dimension of the life he was modeling. Jesus formed a new kind of extended family in the house of Simon and Andrew in Capernaum, welcoming the lost and broken. This became the staging ground from which Jesus trained this group of 72 in mission and then sent them out in pairs to do it. It was a small enough group to feel a strong sense of ownership for the mission being entrusted to them, but it was large enough to provide a sense of strength and support to go out and face this huge challenge. When they returned to gather together again, they celebrated together the amazing things God did through them. Jesus demonstrates that Social Space is best suited for extending the OUT dimension of our lives.

What about Intimate Space in this three-dimensional community that Jesus built? When we look at the instances where Jesus invested separately in his three closest disciples, it becomes clear that this deepest form of community is meant to function in all three dimensions. When Jesus went to raise Jairus' daughter from the dead, one of the most challenging OUT missions he ever undertook, he invited Peter, James, and John (Mark 5:35-43). When Jesus went up on a high mountain where he was transfigured, one of the most mystical UP encounters of his life, he brought this inner circle with him (Mark 9:2-18). When Jesus wrestled with his own fears in the Garden of Gethsemane, he asked these three closest friends to come along for support, perhaps the most intimate expression of Jesus' IN we find in the Gospels (Mark 14:32-33). Intimate Space is the setting where we are able to share all three dimensions of Jesus' life with those we trust the most.

Looking carefully at the way Jesus built community, we can see that, while all four of these Spaces include the three dimensions of his life, each one is especially effective in one of those three dimensions. It looks like this:

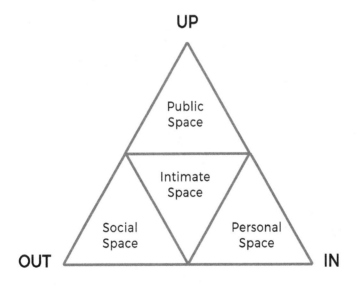

> Jesus built the foundations for healthy and fruitful community by modeling the way life is meant to be lived in all four communal spaces. Not surprisingly, these differing spaces corresponded to the three primary dimensions of Jesus' life.

When my colleague Greg and I first traveled to Sheffield and experienced life with the people of St. Thomas' Church, we both sensed that this was a church more like the one Jesus planted than any we had ever experienced. What we didn't know then was that we were sensing intuitively what I am explaining explicitly here. The people of St. Thomas' Church model their lives, individually and corporately, on the pattern Jesus set.

Their large worship gatherings (Public Space) offer powerful experiences of a God who speaks and moves through his people today, calling for a response of faith. It is fertile ground for growth in the UP dimension. Their small group Huddles (Personal Space) are not simply gatherings of friends to discuss biblical ideas, but places where enough trust is developed to actually speak God's Word into each other's lives as part of a discipling process. They are powerful expressions of the IN dimension. In addition to these familiar types of gatherings, they also are multiplying mid-sized Missional Communities (Social Space) defined by a specific missional purpose, offering both motivation and support for people to actually reach out beyond the church, engage unchurched people where they are, and do with them the things that Jesus did. What an empowering environment for dramatically expanding the OUT dimension!

This approach of intentionally shaping our lives together after the pattern of Jesus' life is what Alan Hirsch and Michael Frost mean when they tell us we need to "Re-Jesus the Church."[9] If we are honest, most of us will have to admit that we have unconsciously allowed our own experience of church to

---

9.   Alan Hirsch, Michael Frost, *ReJesus: A Wild Messiah for a Missional Church* (Peabody: Hendrickson, 2009).

shape our view of Jesus and his mission, rather than the other way around. This explains why our lives and the fruit we produce are so different from the life and fruit of Jesus and those who shaped their lives after his. What if we were to let the shape of Jesus' life and the call he has given us shape the form of our life together?

Hirsch tells us Christology is meant to form our Missiology, which in turn determines our Ecclesiology. Mike Breen explains it this way: "If you make disciples, you always get the church. But if you make a church, you rarely get disciples."[10] This is precisely how Jesus began his world-changing movement. He invested his life in people who would become like him, sent them to carry out his mission in the wider world, and the result was a powerful, dynamic church which even the gates of hell could not overcome!

Jesus not only modeled for us the life we are meant to live individually, but also corporately. In a world of two-dimensional Flatland churches, Jesus invites us to follow him into Spaceland and discover what three-dimensional friendships, a three-dimensional marriage, a three-dimensional family, and a three-dimensional community looks like. If our churches are going to recapture the discipling passion and missional power of the early church, we will need to learn how to lead our large worship gatherings to experience God more powerfully, allowing him to expand the UP dimension of our lives. We will need to form smaller discipling groups that offer both support and challenge, along with practical tools that empower people to genuinely live the IN dimension as Jesus did. We will need to fill in the missing piece of launching mid-sized Missional Commu-

> If we are honest, most of us will have to admit that we have unconsciously allowed our own experience of church to shape our view of Jesus and his mission, rather than the other way around.

---

10. Breen, *Building a Discipling Culture*, p. 11.

nities where our members can recapture ownership and empowerment to live the mission of Jesus in the world, revolutionizing the OUT dimension of our lives. This is the church Jesus invites us to become.

EMPOWERING MISSIONAL DISCIPLES

The three dimensions of Jesus' life and the three-dimensional community he built reflect the three ingredients that made the movement Jesus started so explosive. God is calling us to reclaim these priorities in our lives and our churches today if we are to go back to our roots before Constantine's Edict of Milan and recover the church of Jesus.

Jesus primarily focused his life and his followers on:

> **Biblical Empowerment:** Inviting people to encounter God by living in Covenant with him and with each other, claiming the authority of Jesus' Kingdom, so his transforming power flows through them (UP with the Father)
>
> **Discipling Culture**: Learning how to live the life of Jesus and effectively multiplying this in the lives of others through relational investment (IN with the disciples)
>
> **Missional Community:** Releasing extended families of disciples who support each other to effectively carry out the mission of Jesus in the world (OUT with the world)

We can understand the implications of these three priorities this way:

JESUS' PRIORITIES	DIMENSION OF JESUS' LIFE	RELATIONAL CONTEXT	PRIMARY SPACE
Biblical Empowerment	UP	The Father	Public Space
Discipling Culture	IN	The Disciples	Personal Space
Missional Community	OUT	The World	Social Space

Jesus empowered people to operate in his authority and power through the biblical dynamics of Covenant and Kingdom. He invested his life in a group of disciples and trained them to do what he did. He formed the kind of community where these disciples could work together in carrying out his mission as a way of life. This characterized the explosive movement of early Christianity. Simply put, Jesus *empowered missional disciples*. We must do the same if we are to recover that same passion, face the challenge of postmodernity, and extend God's Kingdom in our day.

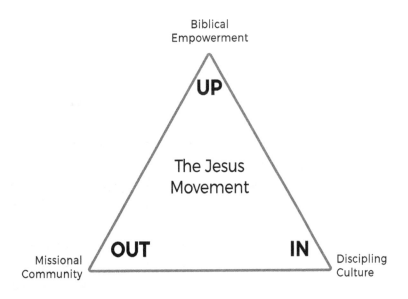

Empowered missional disciples were the primary fruit of Jesus' life. Like all good fruit, these disciples brought life and blessing everywhere they went, and they contained within them the DNA of their source. The seeds of that fruit were scattered across the fertile soil of the Roman Empire, and orchards were planted where these same kind of disciples were rapidly multiplied. Even when this fruit was violently consumed, the ashes of its intended destruction proved to be fertilizer for seeds that produced the ongoing growth of a transformational movement which neither emperors nor gladiators could stop.

As the followers of Jesus began to conform to the mold of Roman society under Constantine, Jesus' DNA became increasingly less evident in their lives. Gradually the movement was co-opted and neutered of its transformational power. But those seeds have lain fallow for many centuries, periodically taking root in places like Assisi, Wittenberg, Aldersgate, and Azusa Street, intermittently producing this same fruit and giving hope for the recovery of the global movement of Jesus. We live in a time of unprecedented opportunity for this DNA to be recovered, for these seeds to be replanted in good soil across the globe, and for the same dynamic movement of missional discipleship that revolutionized the Roman Empire to transform our postmodern world today.

We live in a time of unprecedented opportunity for this DNA to be recovered, for these seeds to be replanted in good soil across the globe, and for the same dynamic movement of missional discipleship that revolutionized the Roman Empire to transform our postmodern world today.

Jesus made an outrageous prediction, *"Very truly I tell you, all who have faith in me will do the works I have been doing, and they will do even greater things than these, because I am going to the Father."* (John 14:12) The DNA of Jesus produces disciples who are becoming like him and who are empowered to carry out his mission in the world. Like a sort of biblical genome project, many have been laboring to unlock this code so we might once again begin to fulfill Jesus' outrageous prediction. The pages that follow are aimed at mapping this Jesus genome by looking more closely at these three key priorities of Jesus: learning to live in biblical empowerment, building a discipling culture, and releasing people in missional communities to bring the Good News of the Kingdom to all people. The goal of this book is that you will become connected to this missional discipling movement so that the DNA of Jesus might be replicated in you and those close to you.[11] Let's continue by looking more closely at where we can find the power we need to do God's will.

---

11. If you plan to implement the things I am writing about, do not try it alone! I recommend joining a 3DM Learning Community or a 3DM Coaching Huddle.

PART 1

THE DNA OF BIBLICAL EMPOWERMENT

6

THE DNA OF THE BIBLE

JESUS AND THE WORD OF GOD

Like every educated Jew of his time, Jesus was deeply steeped in the Scriptures. The Hebrew Bible was the basic curriculum for Jewish school children, and they memorized vast passages as a matter of course. However, Jesus' understanding and use of Scripture was unique. By age twelve he was already conversing with the rabbis who taught at the Temple in Jerusalem. Whenever he preached in the synagogues of Galilee, his hearers were riveted by the authority of his teaching. He was not afraid to flout rabbinical custom in favor of what the Bible actually says. He offered interpretations that had radical implications, both for his hearers and for himself. Clearly, Scripture played a major role in the impact of Jesus' ministry.

Jesus understood the connection between the Word of God and spiritual power. He knew it was by his Word that God created all that exists: *"Let there be..."* (Genesis 1:3). He knew it was by his Word that Yahweh established Covenant with Abraham (Genesis 15:1), instructed the people of Israel in the wilderness (Deuteronomy 5:3-5), awakened the prophetic calling of Samuel (1 Samuel 3:7-10), warned Jerusalem of the coming Babylonian invasion (2 Kings 20:16-17), promised the rebuilding of the Temple in Jerusalem (Ezra 1:1-4), and foretold the coming of a new Covenant (Jeremiah 31:1-34). Not only was Jesus a master at understanding and applying the written Word of God, but he also knew how to hear the revealed word of his Father and simply speak the words he was given. He explained the power of his words this way: *"The words that I say to you I do not speak on my own authority, but the Father who dwells in me does his works."* (John 14:10)

God described the power of his Word this way: *"For as the rain and the snow come down from heaven and do not return there but water the earth, making it bring forth and sprout, giving seed to the sower and bread to the eater, so shall my word be that goes out from my mouth; it shall not return to me empty, but it shall accomplish that which I purpose, and shall succeed in the thing for which I sent it."* (Isaiah 55:10-11) God's Word carries within it the power to accomplish what it declares. John tells us that Jesus is the Word become flesh (John 1:14), so who would know this better than Jesus? When his identity was questioned by the devil in the wilderness, Jesus quoted Scripture in reply each time: *"It is written..."* He knew God's Word is *"living and active, sharper than any two-edged sword"* (Hebrews 4:12).

The reason Jesus was able to speak God's Word with such transforming power was that he was clear about his identity as the Son of God and claimed the authority he was given to represent his Father, the King of the Universe. This unprecedented connection between identity and authority was the key to Jesus' power and obedience, and it flowed from the two central themes that run throughout the entire Bible. When heard together, these two themes speak in a powerful kind of stereophonic sound. We describe these themes using the biblical terms Covenant and Kingdom. In his foundational book, *Covenant and Kingdom: The DNA of the Bible*, Mike Breen works his way through the great canonical narratives from Genesis to Revelation, revealing the dynamic interplay of these two themes.[12] He describes Covenant and Kingdom as the "warp and weft" by which God weaves the tapestry of his redemptive story, the navigational "longitude and latitude" that God uses to guide us on this journey, and the twin double-helix strands of the Bible's essential DNA that replicates its life-giving truth in our lives. As we learn to identify and understand these twin strands, they become the key that unlocks the transforming power of God's Word in our lives as well.

THE DNA OF THE OLD TESTAMENT

Covenant is the biblical term that describes the relationships of love and faithfulness for which God created us—relationships first with him and then with each other. The purpose of Covenant is always to restore the unity or oneness that God intended for us in the beginning, but that was obliterated by sin and all its consequences. Covenant is a relationship in which both parties say to each other, "Everything I am, everything I have, I give to you."

In the original account of Creation, we discover that *"God created man in his own image, in the image of God he created him; male and female he created them."* (Genesis 1:27) The Hebrew word image used here can also be translated imprint. Drawing on the imagery of Genesis 2, we can picture the potter leaving the imprint of his hand in the clay. This imprint is evidence that the

> The reason Jesus was able to speak God's Word with such transforming power was that he was clear about his identity as the Son of God and claimed the authority he was given to represent his Father, the King of the Universe.

---

12. Mike Breen, Covenant and Kingdom (Pawley's Island, 3DM Publishing, 2010).

vessel is designed for unity with its Maker, because only the potter's hand will fill the void of that imprint.

The second strand of biblical DNA is Kingdom, which describes the responsibility God has given us to represent him. The purpose of Kingdom is always to accomplish God's will for his children and all of creation. When God created us in his image, he also gave us this mandate, *"Be fruitful and multiply and fill the earth and subdue it, and have dominion over the fish of the sea and over the birds of the heavens and over every living thing that moves on the earth"* (Genesis 1:28). This was not license to exploit the earth for our own ends, but authority and responsibility to represent God by acting on his behalf and carrying out his will as stewards of his creation. In the next chapter, we see the man already fulfilling this role as he gets to work tending the garden and naming the animals (Genesis 2:15-20).

The perfection of Eden was a reflection of Adam and Eve living in faithful Covenant with God and each other, while also faithfully living out their Kingdom calling. When Adam and Eve violated Covenant with God by usurping his role and trying to live independently of him, the intimate connection of Covenant was broken, and the productive mandate of Kingdom was forfeited. The result was separation, frustration, and shame. This is the great tragedy of human history—we lost our unity with the Creator and our community with each other, while forfeiting our role to represent God by ruling Creation on his behalf.

In the cool of the evening, the Creator came searching for his children, *"Where are you?"* Our Father's longing voice still echoes down the corridors of time, calling us out of hiding and back into Covenant with him. Tragically, Adam traded the fruitfulness of princely rule for the curse of sweaty toil and a dusty grave: *"It will produce thorns and thistles."* Demonstrating the inadequacy of their attempted cover-up, God covered their shame with animal skins instead of leaves, the first sign of death in the Creation account. Through the shedding of blood, which in biblical terms means the giving of life, God was beginning the long journey of drawing us back into Covenant union with him and restoring our role as his earthly representatives.

As we read through the Old Testament, we see these themes of Covenant and Kingdom in the accounts of Noah, Abraham, Joseph, Moses, and David. Each was called back into relationship with God in different ways in order to begin to represent him by carrying out his will in a specific chapter of the cosmic story. Some offer us a clearer example of the Covenant strand of biblical DNA, while others model the Kingdom strand more clearly.

Abraham's story epitomizes Covenant, as he receives God's promise of land, descendants, and relationship, and seals it by walking through the blood of his sacrifice (Genesis 15:1-21). This Covenant relationship with God becomes the basis for the covenantal people of Israel and ultimately the New Covenant in Jesus.

Joseph, on the other hand, is the poster child for the Kingdom strand of biblical DNA. Through the trials of slavery, false accusation, and imprisonment, Joseph learned to allow God to reign at the center of his universe. Joseph learned to represent God and his will, rather than himself. As a result, in fulfillment of his own prophetic dreams, Joseph was raised up to rule Egypt in order that God's redemptive purpose might be accomplished (Genesis 37-50).

In Moses, for the first time, we see both Covenant and Kingdom explicitly revealed. God made a Covenant with Moses by revealing his own personal name in the burning bush and promising to be with him. Then God called Moses to represent him in challenging Pharaoh and leading his people from slavery back into the Promised Land (Exodus 4-14). On the basis of his Covenant with the God who is greater than the Pharaohs of Egypt, this middle-aged shepherd was able to single-handedly face down the greatest superpower of his day and lead a multitude of slaves out of bondage into the freedom of God's promise. This is what happens when we learn to live in both Covenant and Kingdom!

Throughout the Hebrew Scriptures, we see these twin dynamics of Covenant and Kingdom leading God's people from relationship with him to representing him to the rest of the world. As God says through the prophet Isaiah, *"I am the LORD, I have called you in righteousness, I have taken you by the hand and kept you; I have given you as a covenant to the people, a light to the nations, to open the eyes that are blind, to bring out the prisoners from the dungeon, from the prison those who sit in darkness."* (Isaiah 42:6-7) All those who live in Covenant relationship with God will be given the power to shine the light of his coming Kingdom to a dark and dying world.

THE DNA OF THE NEW TESTAMENT

As we move from the Old Testament to the New, we find Jesus described as both Son of God, emphasizing his Covenant unity with the Father, and Son of Man, emphasizing his role of representing the rule of God on earth. When Jesus was baptized by John in the Jordan River, his covenantal relationship with the Father was clearly expressed by the voice from heaven that said, *"You are my beloved Son; with you I am well pleased"* (Mark 1:11). Then Jesus was led into the wilderness, where he overcame the temptation to represent himself or Satan, instead of representing God's rule, as he quoted from Deuteronomy, *"Worship the Lord your God, and him only shall you serve"* (Matthew 4:10). When Jesus launched his ministry he announced the critical time had come for *"the good news"* and *"the Kingdom of God"* to be fully revealed (Mark 1:15).

> Throughout the Hebrew Scriptures, we see these twin dynamics of Covenant and Kingdom leading God's people from relationship with him to representing him to the rest of the world.

The Good News Jesus proclaimed was an invitation to Covenant relationship with God so close we can know him as our own

"Abba" (Daddy) and address God as *"our Father"* the way Jesus did (Matthew 6:9; Mark 14:36). Jesus lived out this Covenant by investing his life in a community of disciples, giving them his name, his Kingdom, and his very life. While celebrating his final Passover meal with them, Jesus explained the basis of this defining relationship, *"This cup is the new covenant in my blood, which is poured out for you"* (Luke 22:14-20). The very next day, this promise was fulfilled by the spilling of his blood on the cross. When he rose from the dead, the resurrected Jesus showed the wounds in his hands to the disciples, sealing an eternal Covenant of grace foretold by Isaiah, *"See, I have engraved you on the palms of my hands"* (Isaiah 49:16; Luke 24:36-40).

The Kingdom Jesus announced was one where he both taught us to pray for God's will to be done *"on earth as it is in heaven"* (Matthew 6:10), and also showed us how to become conduits of the power required to accomplish that redemptive purpose (Luke 10:1-21). Jesus constantly modeled the Kingdom of God by miraculously feeding the multitudes, healing the sick, releasing the oppressed, and raising the dead. Jesus passed this Kingdom on to those who lived in Covenant with him, empowering them to do the very same things (Luke 9:1). When Jesus cried *"It is finished"* from the cross, it was his victory cry announcing the triumph of God's Kingdom over sin, death, hell, and the devil (John 19:28-30). When Jesus rose from the dead, it was irrefutable proof that the victory was indeed won, and God's Kingdom would continue to come with power.

The followers of Jesus were empowered to do the things Jesus did, not only while he was with them physically, but even after his ascension into heaven when they were filled with the Holy Spirit. Peter, who received Jesus' name in Covenant along with the keys to his Kingdom, stood up in Jerusalem on the day of Pentecost and proclaimed the New Covenant through Jesus' death and resurrection (Acts 2:14-41). Three thousand accepted the invitation!

> The Kingdom Jesus announced was one where he both taught us to pray for God's will to be done *"on earth as it is in heaven"* (Matthew 6:10), and also showed us how to become conduits of the power required to accomplish that redemptive purpose (Luke 10:1-21).

Not long after that, Peter and John met the crippled man at the Beautiful Gate on the Temple Mount and *"in the name of Jesus Christ of Nazareth"* they commanded him to *"rise up and walk"* (Acts 3:6). The man did them one better and began to dance, inspiring five thousand to put their faith in Jesus! Not only Peter, but all the followers of Jesus were empowered to do God's will on earth in a way they never could have before. Living in Covenant with God and each other, the unstoppable power of God's Kingdom flowed through them as representatives of Jesus and continued to flow through those in whom they invested their lives.

7

THE SECRET OF JESUS' EXTRAORDINARY LIFE

PLUGGING IN

When I was a kid, my dad graciously allowed me to use any of the hand tools on his workbench, but the power tools were understandably forbidden. You can do a lot with a handsaw, hammer, and screwdriver, but there

are obvious limits. Flower boxes and birdhouses are cool, but I was drawn to the turned walnut candlesticks and the cherry colonial china cabinet my grandfather had created in his basement workshop. I ran my fingers over the curving surfaces of gleaming hardwood and marveled about how he crafted such wonders.

I vividly remember the day my grandfather invited me into his basement and introduced me to the world of power tools. "This," he said, "is a table saw. You can do almost anything with it, and it can do almost anything to you." As carefully as a diamond-cutter taking hold of a raw stone, he took a chunk of oak, adjusted the rip fence, flipped the switch on the ancient saw, and firmly guided the oak through the blade, producing a perfectly straight and parallel cut in the hard wood. Wide-eyed with fear and wonder, I began to understand the potential of these powerful tools.

My grandpa soon schooled me in the use of the joiner, the band saw, the drill press, the shaper, and my favorite, the lathe. With each one he showed me how to adjust the settings, operate the levers, and hold the wood. And then he flipped the switch. The machine began to whir, and sawdust started to fly. I loved descending into that basement shop crammed with every imaginable tool. The smell of hardwood blending with machine oil was to me an intoxicating blend because it spoke of the creative masterpieces these tools could produce—all with the flip of a switch. But if you cut off the electricity to that magical workshop, everything would come to a screeching halt. None of those tools could produce anything of value if they didn't have enough power.

Of course, the same is true of the things God has called us to. It's fine to rediscover Jesus' invitation to become and make disciples, but where do we get the power to do the things he did? The call to form communities who live out Jesus' mission in the world sounds good, but how do we empower people to move out of their comfort zones and actually do it? When we hear Jesus' call to *"drive out all demons and to cure diseases... to proclaim the kingdom of God and to heal the sick"* (Luke 9:1-2), we smile politely. But inside we know we will never do it, because obviously that is stuff that only Jesus has the power to do.

Or is it?

WHAT KIND OF JESUS?

I have always been fascinated by movies about Jesus because they often tell us more about the filmmakers than they do about Jesus. Film leaves little to the imagination, so the makers of a film have to supply all those details that the Gospels leave out. I've made it a point to watch as many different types of Jesus films as I can find and, from my perspective, they generally fall into two types of portrayals. Older films tend to picture a very divine Jesus, floating across the landscape of Palestine, seemingly impervious to dust or wind, every hair sprayed carefully into place. He's almost like a mystical Miss America, complete with the blue sash across his robe! This type of Jesus is a magic man who is able to defy gravity and perform powerful miracles by virtue of his singular distinctiveness. He is obviously a being like none other, and no one could hope to do what he does.

More recent Jesus films tend to portray a much more human Jesus. This Messiah is a kindly soul with lots of folk wisdom and a soft spot for children. Alternately, he is a slightly unstable revolutionary filled with self-doubt and ready to fly off the handle at any moment. Either way, he appears to perform miracles, but these are really just an illusion created by overly enthusiastic followers, fortuitous misunderstandings, or even Jesus' own sleight of hand. In actuality this kind of Jesus has no more power than a really clever college professor.

Obviously, both of these genres miss the mark. That's why early theologians fought so hard to defend the Christological paradox that many wanted to resolve one way or the other—Jesus is, at the same time, both fully human and fully divine. It is so easy to fall off one side of that horse or the other, but the key to really getting Jesus is to keep your balance by accepting the paradoxical tension of these seemingly opposite realities. Many today have lost sight of Jesus' divinity, but those of us who believe in the truth of Jesus' miracles as recorded by eyewitness Gospel accounts tend to make the opposite mistake — losing sight of Jesus' humanity.

For most of my Christian life, I assumed Jesus could perform miracles because he was God. The obvious implication of that assumption is that I cannot perform miracles since (thankfully) I am not God. This mindset is shared by most followers of Jesus today. The only problem with this assumption is that Jesus assumed the opposite. He called people to follow him as his disciples, which meant he believed they could learn how to do what he did.

Jesus sent out his followers with the specific command to perform the same kind of miracles he did. I don't know what the disciples' assumptions were prior to going out on this mission, but they came back knowing from first-hand experience that my assumption is wrong. They could and did do what Jesus did—including proclamation, healing, and deliverance.

The problem we run into when it comes to keeping the full humanity of Jesus in perspective is that he continually does things only God can do: feeding the multitudes with five fish sandwiches, making blind people see, crippled people walk, vanquishing legions of demons, calming storms, walking on water, and even raising the dead. At one level it's understandable for us to jump to the conclusion that Jesus is really more divine than human—but only because we have somehow forgotten Jesus never claimed to do these things in and of himself. In fact, he said repeatedly, *"By myself I can do nothing"* (John 5:30), always pointing to his Covenantal relationship with the Father as the key to his Kingdom authority and power.

> Many today have lost sight of Jesus' divinity, but those of us who believe in the truth of Jesus' miracles as recorded by eyewitness Gospel accounts tend to make the opposite mistake – losing sight of Jesus' humanity.

Paul quotes a creed of the earliest church which helps us understand this mystery: *"Christ Jesus, who, though he was in the form of God, did not count equality with God a thing to be grasped, but emptied himself, by taking the form of a servant, being born in the likeness of men. And being found in human form, he humbled himself by becoming obedient to the point of death, even death on a cross."* (Philippians 2:5-8) The Greek word translated emptied himself is *kenosis*, which describes a process of pouring oneself out for another.

This does not sound like a magic man who can do anything because he possesses divine powers that we mere mortals could never attain. Nor does it sound like Jesus' power was some kind of clever trick or illusion. *Kenosis* does not mean that Jesus stopped being God when he became human, but it does mean that God chose to limit the expression of his full divinity during Jesus' life on earth. This means Jesus is the example which we can follow by virtue of our relationship with the Father. If we are going to have a truly biblical Christology, then we must embrace a Jesus who is fully human as we are and yet is able to do things that only God can do—not as an exception to the rest of humanity, but as a model for the rest of us.

LESSONS IN JESUS' POWER

So how did Jesus do it? Jesus lived a relatively unremarkable life up until the age of 30. At that point he decided to receive baptism from John in the Jordan River. This event marked the beginning of Jesus' remarkable ministry, and it helps us understand how he operated in divine power while being fully human like us.

Mark begins his account of Jesus' life by describing his baptism: the heavens were torn open, the Holy Spirit was poured out on Jesus, and his Heavenly Father spoke: *"You are my Son, whom I love; with you I am well pleased"* (Mark 1:11). It's hard to imagine a clearer or more convincing revelation of Jesus' true identity as Son of the Father.

After Jesus' baptism *"the Spirit sent him out into the wilderness"* to face forty days of fasting, trials, and temptations (Mark 1:12-13). We can easily imagine how this might not have been Jesus' first choice of post-baptismal

activities, but he faithfully followed the Spirit's leading anyway. Jesus' identity was naturally expressed by his obedience. When you come to know that you are a child of the Father, the desire grows inside of you to be faithful to your Father's will.

Later Jesus' resolve to obey was tested at an even greater level in the Garden of Gethsemane. *"Abba, Father,"* he said, *"everything is possible for you. Take this cup from me. Yet not what I will, but what you will."* (Mark 14:36) Even in the face of unimaginable suffering and death, Jesus chose obedience as an expression of his relationship with the Father. The writer of Hebrews described the progression this way: *"During the days of Jesus' life on earth, he offered up prayers and petitions with fervent cries and tears to the one who could save him from death, and he was heard because of his reverent submission. Son though he was, he learned obedience from what he suffered and, once made perfect, he became the source of eternal salvation for all who obey him"* (Hebrews 5:7-9). Jesus lived as a perfectly obedient Son because he knew so well who he really was.

Just ten verses after Mark's account of Jesus' baptism, he describes Jesus teaching in the synagogue at Capernaum. The various reactions of his hearers point to the significance of Jesus' identity revealed in his baptism, *"The people were amazed at his teaching, because he taught them as one who had authority, not as the teachers of the law."* One of the reactions to this startling authority came from a demon-possessed man who cried out, *"What do you want with us, Jesus of Nazareth? Have you come to destroy us? I know who you are—the Holy One of God!"* Jesus' response was simple and straightforward, *"Be quiet!" said Jesus sternly. "Come out of him!"* As soon as Jesus left the synagogue, he went to Peter's nearby home and proceeded to heal Peter's fevered mother-in-law. This display of power led to an entire evening of healing and deliverance. Mark concludes by noting that *"He also drove out many demons, but he would not let the demons speak because they knew who he was."* (Mark 1:21-34)

> If we are going to have a truly biblical Christology, then we must embrace a Jesus who is fully human as we are and yet is able to do things that only God can do—not as an exception to the rest of humanity, but as a model for the rest of us.

Though we may have overlooked it in the past, we see here a clear connection between Jesus' identity and the authority in which he operated. Notice how demons always wanted to comment on Jesus' identity, saying things like, *"I know who you are!"* They were aware of the authority Jesus received from his Father, and it terrified them into submission. God is the King of the Universe. Jesus is the Son of God. That means Jesus' identity carries with it unlimited royal authority.

James tells us that demons shudder at the very thought of God's authority (James 2:19). In Jesus' time of testing in the wilderness, the devil himself tried to question Jesus' identity by prefacing his temptation with the phrase, *"If you are the Son of God…"* (Matthew 4:6). The devil knew that if he could get Jesus to question his own identity then he could undermine his authority and so destroy him. However, fresh from the revelation of his identity in baptism and deeply rooted in the written Word of God, Jesus was able to banish the devil himself, saying *"Away from me Satan!"* (Matthew 4:10) and then quoting Scripture.

Authority is intrinsically connected to power. When you are given authority, you are given the power to act on the behalf of another. You can tell who has functional authority in a church by who has been given keys to the facility. When we give someone a set of keys, we are entrusting them with the authority to open and close the building on behalf of the congregation. That authority confers power. When you have the keys, you have the power to open doors or lock them shut.

In secular communities we entrust certain people with the authority to enforce the laws that protect our common good. To symbolize that authority, we issue them a badge. To empower them to act on our behalf, we issue them a gun. Ideally, when

someone is acting contrary to the good of the community, the ones we have authorized will confront them, first by showing their badge to clarify that they are acting on behalf of the community. Then they will show their gun to demonstrate they actually have the power to enact the will of that community. Although we are painfully aware of the frequency with which this public trust is violated through the abuse of authority and power, it doesn't change the fact that we need those who will faithfully exercise both with justice on behalf of the common good. Jesus shows us the same is true in the spiritual realm. When the Father proclaimed Jesus' identity, he was giving him the badge. When Jesus claimed that authority, he received the gun. That is why the demons were so afraid of him—he carried both the Father's badge and gun!

This intrinsic connection between authority and power enabled the fully-human Jesus to do things only God can do. The source of Jesus' power on earth was not his uniquely divine nature as the third Person of the Trinity, important as that is. Remember, God emptied himself in the process of incarnation. The source of Jesus' earthly authority and power flowed from his revealed identity as Son of the Father. Jesus understood that he was the Son of God and that his Abba was the King of the Universe. Therefore Jesus received the royal authority conferred by that Sonship.

> Authority is intrinsically connected to power. When you are given authority, you are given the power to act on the behalf of another.

This distinction is critical because it helps us understand how to receive the authority and power that Jesus confers on those who follow him. Obviously, we are not divine like Jesus, but we share in the same identity revealed in Jesus, because we are also children of God. The reason Jesus commanded us to follow his example in baptism was to demonstrate our true identity as God's beloved daughters and sons. Remember how Jesus taught us to address God in prayer, *"Our Father in heaven"* (Matthew 6:9). It is out of this identity that our desire to obey the will of our Father grows. As Jesus' model prayer goes on, *"your kingdom come, your will be done, on earth as it is in heaven"* (Matthew 6:10). Those who know themselves to be children of the heavenly Father will naturally seek to do his will on earth as it is in heaven.

Because we share Jesus' identity as sons and daughters of God, Jesus is able to pass on to us the same kind of authority to function in God's power which he received. Luke describes how Jesus sent out the twelve to do what he did: *"When Jesus had called the Twelve together, he gave them power and authority to drive out all demons and to cure diseases, and he sent them out to proclaim the kingdom of God and to heal the sick."* (Luke 9:1-2) Isn't it amazing that Jesus' disciples were able to do the same powerful things their Rabbi did! Don't assume this was an exclusive privilege of Jesus' twelve closest disciples. The same authority and power was also extended to the group of 72 disciples who returned saying, *"Lord, even the demons submit to us in your name"* (Luke 10:17).

Doing things in someone else's name means you have been authorized by that person to act on their behalf. Jesus' name was the badge he gave his disciples so they could act on his behalf and do the things he modeled for them. When they stepped out in faith and began to proclaim the Kingdom, heal people, and cast out demons, they didn't try to do it in their own strength or wisdom, but by the authority Jesus had given them—in his name. The result was that the same divine power for good that flowed through Jesus flowed through them to give faith, heal, and liberate. Jesus gives that same badge and gun to anyone today who, by faith, will claim his name in Covenant love and submit to his Kingdom leading through the Holy Spirit.

> Jesus understood that he was the Son of God and that his Abba was the King of the Universe. Therefore Jesus received the royal authority conferred by that Sonship.

This helps us understand what Jesus meant when he said, *"I will do whatever you ask in my name, so that the Father may be glorified in the Son. You may ask me for anything in my name, and I will do it."* (John 14:13-14) He is not suggesting that tacking the phrase in Jesus' name to the end of our prayers will give us omnipotence. Jesus is simply explaining that, because of the Covenantal relationship with our heavenly Father which he makes possible, he gives us the authority to act on his behalf *(in my name)*. Jesus promises that when we claim this authority by faith, God will give us the power to carry out his will *(I will do it)*. We need to learn how to claim the authority Jesus has given us so we can obey our Father's will with the same power that Jesus did. So let's take a closer look at how Jesus accomplished the amazing things he did.

8

OUR IDENTITY AND GOD'S AUTHORITY

WHAT'S IN A NAME?

When Pam was pregnant with our first child, she knew what the name would be if it was a boy. I was named after my father, and she wanted our son to carry that same name. So months before he was born, we knew our son would be named Robert Phillip Rognlien, III. When Pam was pregnant with our second child, she was less decisive. Her water broke, labor started, and we still didn't have a name picked out. I remember driving to the hospital, my mind swirling with inexpressible emotions, but all I could think about was the fact that our soon-to-arrive baby did not have a name.

I think Pam assumed that once she saw our newborn child she would know the right name. It wasn't until the next morning that we agreed to name our new little guy Luke, and I felt like we finally knew who our son was.

One of our most primal instincts is to claim an identity. When a child is born, the inevitable questions come: "Boy or girl? How big? What's the name?" We ask these questions because we are trying to identify who this new child is. We are trying to define their identity. Adolescence is a season in life when we begin to wrestle with the identity we have been given. At twelve years old, our best friends' daughter decided to change her name from Alexandra to Addy. Every time I saw her, I exclaimed, "Hi Alexand ... um Addy," only to be greeted by a dark scowl on her pretty face. It took months for me to finally get it into my head that she was Addy and not Alexandra. Just about that time, she decided to go with "Ally" instead. Twenty years later I still find myself stumbling over her name.

We all need to sort out who we really are. This need often drives us to pursue all kinds of things we subconsciously hope will give us a meaningful sense of identity. We dress a certain way, drive a certain kind of car, live in a certain neighborhood, land a certain job, marry a certain person, acquire certain possessions, and accomplish certain goals, all to tell the world who we are. But as Jesus pointed out, we cannot be defined by our abundance of possessions. None of this has any effect on our identity. There is only one who can tell us who we really are.

As we noted in the previous chapter, Jesus' public ministry began at the River Jordan with God the Father declaring from heaven who Jesus really is: *"my beloved Son."* This is significant because God is the one who created us and knows us fully, and as such he is the one most qualified to tell us who we really are. Jesus submitted to baptism so we might follow in his footsteps. When we are baptized, God declares the same thing over us: "You are my beloved daughter! You are my beloved son! I am so proud of you!" God is the only one who can tell you who you really are, and he has spoken.

This is not just wishful thinking or theological gymnastics. Jesus was very clear about what he was doing when he went to the cross. Just before he was arrested, he reinterpreted the age-old meaning of the Passover meal by saying, *"This cup that is poured out for you is the new covenant in my blood"* (Luke 22:20). As he drew his final breath, he cried out, *"It is finished"* (John 19:30).

> As Jesus pointed out, we cannot be defined by our abundance of possessions. None of this has any effect on our identity. There is only one who can tell us who we really are.

When Jesus rose from the dead, he declared to his disciples, *"I am ascending to my Father and your Father, to my God and your God"* (John 20:17). Jesus' death and resurrection have sealed for us what God foretold through the Prophet Jeremiah: *"Behold, the days are coming, declares the Lord, when I will make a new covenant with the house of Israel and the house of Judah, not like the covenant that I made with their fathers... I will put my law within them, and I will write it on their hearts. And I will be their God, and they shall be my people. And no longer shall each one teach his neighbor and each his brother, saying, 'Know the Lord,' for they shall all know me, from the least of them to the greatest, declares the Lord. For I will forgive their iniquity, and I will remember their sin no more."* (Jeremiah 31:31-34)

Through the cross and the empty tomb, Jesus has established this New Covenant relationship with us, restoring our true identity as God's beloved sons and daughters. We can know who we really are through the love of our Heavenly Father who made us, knows us, saved us, and is calling us to himself. As we come to trust that God really is our Abba and believe we really are his beloved daughters and sons, the desire to do God's will begins to grow inside of us. In a Covenant relationship, obedience is not a heavy burden of obligation, but a light yoke joyfully accepted. John describes the implications of Covenant: *"See what great love the Father has lavished on us, that we should be called children of God! And that is what we are! The reason the world does not know us is that it did not know him. Dear friends, now we are children of God, and what we will be has not yet been made known. But we know that when Christ appears, we shall be like him, for we shall see him as he is. All who have this hope in him purify themselves, just as he is pure."* (1 John 3:1-3)

FINDING WHO WE ARE

We can picture how Covenant works in our lives, using the three dimensions of Jesus' life as a framework. [13]

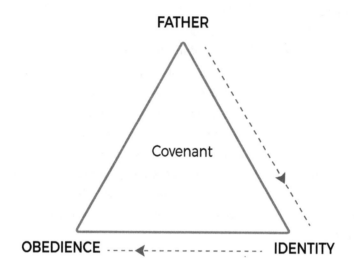

In the UP dimension, we see how Jesus reveals God to us as our Heavenly Father. The Father speaks his Word of grace and love over us, giving us our true identity as his daughters and sons. This is represented by the IN dimension, because now we are part of a new kind of community—the family of God, where we live as brothers and sisters, and where we find spiritual parents, children, and grandchildren. All of this leads us naturally to the OUT dimension, where we desire to do the will of our Father who loves us and begin learning how to live in obedience to his perfect will.

---

13. Breen, *Covenant and Kingdom,* Appendix A.

One of the pitfalls of seeking identity is the lie that we can establish our identity through obedience. Sincere believers throughout the ages have tried to find their identity and worth in God's sight by trying to please and obey him. Whether it was a Pharisee named Saul of Tarsus zealously guarding the Law by persecuting the first followers of Jesus, or an Augustinian monk named Martin Luther flagellating himself in a German monastery, the result is always the same: religious legalism.

These saints who have gone before have conclusively demonstrated it is impossible to obey our way to the Father. Faith in the grace of Jesus is the only way our identity can be restored, and submission is the way genuine obedience can begin. Paul explains: *For it is by grace you have been saved, through faith—and this is not from yourselves, it is the gift of God— not by works, so that no one can boast. For we are God's handiwork, created in Christ Jesus to do good works, which God prepared in advance for us to do."* (Ephesians 2:8-10)

We can picture these two differing paths to identity and obedience this way:

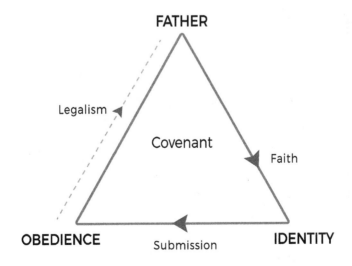

> These saints who have gone before have conclusively demonstrated it is impossible to obey our way to the Father. Faith in the grace of Jesus is the only way our identity can be restored, and submission is the way genuine obedience can begin.

Legalism is always a dead-end street. It falls short of establishing our true identity every time. The grace and mercy of the New Covenant which Jesus made possible through his death and resurrection is the only way for us to discover who we really are. By faith in Jesus we are adopted as God's daughters and sons for all eternity.

Paul experienced this for himself and described it this way: "But when the set time had fully come, God sent his Son, born of a woman, born under the law, to redeem those under the law, that we might receive adoption to sonship. Because you are his sons, God sent the Spirit of his Son into our hearts, the Spirit who calls out, 'Abba, Father.' So you are no longer a slave, but God's child; and since you are his child, God has made you also an heir." (Galatians 4:4-7) In this Covenant of grace, God has adopted you as his own daughter or son. As his child, the Holy Spirit is calling you to live the life you were meant to live in relationship to your heavenly Father. In this relationship you have been promised an inheritance: the present and coming Kingdom of God.

OUR INHERITANCE

During World War II, my grandfather, Gordon, served in the U.S. Army as an attorney based in San Francisco. One day after the war ended, a school buddy called him from his home state of Montana to say that he and a mutual friend were buying side-by-side lots on magnificent Flathead Lake. Sight unseen my Grandpa bought 100 feet of lakefront property that day. Returning home to his wife Myrna and their young kids, Gordon began to build a cabin on that property. Ever since it has been the special place where our family has spent our summer vacations.

I grew up each summer swimming in those crystal clear waters by day and staring up at innumerable stars by night, just like my grandfather and father before me. For the past twenty-five years, my sons have done the same, and we look forward to welcoming a fifth generation into this great family blessing. As responsibility for the lake property passed to my generation, I realized how important it was to make sure this great inheritance gets passed on to successive generations. What a  shame it would be if we fumbled the ball and my grandchildren and great-grandchildren never had a chance to enjoy what was passed on to us by virtue of our identity as children and grandchildren of Gordon and Myrna.

Some things belong to us simply because of who we are. This is especially true for the children of God. Our Covenant inheritance as daughters and sons of God is what Jesus simply called the Kingdom of God. As Jesus promised, *"Seek his kingdom, and these things will be added to you. Fear not, little flock, for it is your Father's good pleasure to give you the kingdom."* (Luke 12:31-32) The Kingdom is God's reign enacted; it is the way things are when God's will is being done on earth as it is in heaven. Covenant is always meant to lead us into the Kingdom. As we come to realize our Daddy is in fact the King of the Universe, the implications of our identity become clearer. We begin to understand that sons and daughters of the King are given royal authority. This authority gives us access to the power required to carry out the King's orders.

Again, using the three dimensions of Jesus' life, we picture the relationship between Authority and Power in God's Kingdom this way:

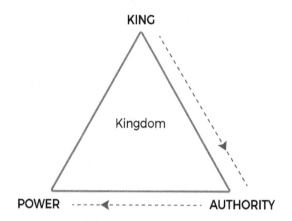

In the UP dimension, Jesus shows us our Covenant Father is also the King of kings, Lord of lords, Ruler of the Universe, the One who holds all authority and power. We know that the sons and daughters of earthly kings carry the authority of their father simply because of who they are. The same is true of God's children. The IN dimension shows us our identity as children of God and means we have been given authority to represent our Father the King. As we claim that authority by faith in the OUT dimension, God's power begins to flow through us, and we are able to do things we otherwise never could do.

The reason Jesus was able to do God's will on earth as it is in heaven was that he claimed the authority given to him by his Father. From this authority flowed the divine power to feed the hungry, heal the sick, make the lame walk, and cause the blind to see. Jesus explicitly passed on this authority and power to his followers so they could also do their Father's will. It is critically important to remember the authority we are talking about is God's authority, entrusted to us by Jesus to do his will and not our own. The power of God's Kingdom only comes when we are submitted to his authority and not trying to claim it for our own ends.

In the book of Acts we read about the seven sons of a Jewish chief priest named Sceva who were trying to operate in the authority of Jesus even though they were not in Covenant with him. The problem with this was the authority they were exercising was really their own and not his. Luke tells us these sons of Sceva were trying to cast out demons by saying, "*'In the name of the Jesus whom Paul preaches, I command you to come out.' One day the evil spirit answered them, 'Jesus I know, and Paul I know about, but who are you?' Then the man who had the evil spirit jumped on them and over-powered them all. He gave them such a beating that they ran out of the house naked and bleeding.*" (Acts 19:13-16)

This is a humorous but cautionary tale, reminding us that Kingdom power flows out of Covenant relationship. The problem with the sons of Sceva is they were not in Covenant with Jesus and were trying to use his name for their own ends. If we are in Covenant with God through Jesus, we will seek his will above our own and learn to operate in his authority, not ours. On the foundation of this kind of Covenant relationship, God can begin to build his Kingdom. Without that foundation we are simply building our own kingdoms that are destined to come crashing down. If seeking our identity with the Father through our own obedience is a dead-end street, exercising spiritual power on the basis of our own authority is downright dangerous. In fact this kind of self-serving exercise of power always constitutes manipulation:

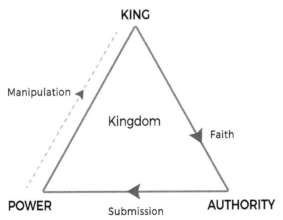

> The reason Jesus was able to do God's will on earth as it is in heaven was that he claimed the authority given to him by his Father. From this authority flowed the divine power to feed the hungry, heal the sick, make the lame walk, and cause the blind to see.

Faith is the way we claim the authority that has already been given to us, and submission is the way that authority leads to spiritual power. When we trust that Jesus really has given us all authority on heaven and earth, and we begin to step out in faith by seeking his will as an exercise of that authority, God's power starts to flow through us. Those who try to exercise spiritual power on their own authority inevitably end up manipulating others by imposing their own will under the guise of doing God's will. This quickly creates a coercive culture where spiritual abuse can abound. Rather than Spirit-led empowerment for the sake of others, this is a flesh-based exercise of power over others for selfish ends. One of the primary reasons some people see the exercise of spiritual power as intrinsically negative is because this is the kind of dynamic they have experienced or imagined. There is no room for this kind of manipulative power in Jesus' Kingdom.

One of the clear marks of Jesus' Kingdom is transformational power manifested in spite of, and even because of, human weakness. In Jesus, God set aside his power and majesty, taking on the frailty of human flesh. Jesus' greatest exercise of power was the redemption of all things accomplished in his moment of greatest weakness, his death on the cross. The apostle Paul well understood this through his own experience of a thorn in the flesh. He says, *"Three times I pleaded with the Lord about this, that it should leave me. But he said to me, 'My grace is sufficient for you, for my power is made perfect in weakness.' Therefore I will boast all the more gladly of my weaknesses, so that the power of Christ may rest upon me."* (2 Corinthians 12:8-9)

The power of God's Kingdom does not flow through those who rely on their own strength or authority. This kind of life-giving power flows most effectively through those who admit their own weakness, submit to the leading of the Holy Spirit, and learn to claim Jesus' authority in faith to do God's will and not their own. The most powerful Kingdom leaders are those who know exactly where the power lies and who gets all the glory. This is why Paul, so open about all his shortcomings, weaknesses, and failings, was such an effective conduit of God's transforming power.

Receiving authority and power from Jesus raises the question, how are we to pass this on to others?

> When we trust that Jesus really has given us all authority on heaven and earth, and we begin to step out in faith by seeking his will as an exercise of that authority, God's power starts to flow through us.

9

PASSING ON BIBLICAL EMPOWERMENT

THE SOURCE OF KINGDOM POWER

Jesus was clear that the Kingdom movement he began would be carried forward through the leadership of those he discipled in Covenantal community, through those whom they discipled in the same way, and so on. In the extended prayer he offered on their behalf the night before his arrest, Jesus prayed to his Father, *"As you sent me into the world, so I have sent them into the world... I do not ask for these only, but also for those who will believe in me through their word, that they may all be one, just as you, Father, are in me, and I in you, that they also may be in us, so that the world may believe that you have sent me."* (John 17:18-21) Jesus prayed that their Covenant oneness with God and each other would continue to grow, so God's Kingdom power would continue to flow through those who in turn followed them.

But when Jesus told them he was going away that night, the disciples were deeply troubled, because they knew it was impossible for them to exercise God's power apart from Jesus. He assured them they would not be abandoned in their ongoing Kingdom calling. Jesus promised he would continue to be with them in an even closer Covenantal relationship through the outpouring of the Holy Spirit that was to come: *"I will ask the Father, and he will give you another Helper, to be with you forever, even the Spirit of truth, whom the world cannot receive, because it neither sees him nor knows him. You know him, for he dwells with you and will be in you. I will not leave you as orphans; I will come to you."* (John 14:16-18)

When Jesus' identity was first revealed in his baptism, this identification included a visible sign of the Holy Spirit being poured out upon him. Jesus promised the disciples that a similar experience would enable them to extend his Covenant and Kingdom to the whole world. Just before ascending into heaven, he said, *"But you will receive power when the Holy Spirit has come upon you, and you will be my witnesses in Jerusalem and in all Judea and Samaria, and to the end of the earth."* (Acts 1:8)

The fulfillment of this promise on the Day of Pentecost marks the beginning of a movement no longer bounded by the limitations of an incarnate Jesus, but filled with the limitless potential of the empowering presence of God alive in each and every person living in Covenant with him. Jesus described it this way: *"On that day you will realize that I am in my Father, and you are in me, and I am in you"* (John 14:20). This realization of the resurrected Jesus' continuing presence in the lives of his followers emboldened them to keep claiming his authority and exercising his power long after he departed from them physically.

The New Testament is clear that all who claim the name of Jesus in Covenant relationship with the Father have the Holy Spirit living inside of them (John 14:15-20; 1 Corinthians 12:3). Those who have also let go of control and learned to live in the Kingdom by the empowerment of that same Spirit are described as being *"filled with the Spirit"* (Luke 1:41; Acts 4:31). Paul made it clear this is an ongoing journey when he said, *"Do not get drunk on wine, which leads to debauchery. Instead, be filled with the Spirit."* (Ephesians 5:18) The Greek verb translated *be filled* here has a continuative sense; i.e. *keep on being filled*. The journey from Covenant identity and obedience to Kingdom authority and power is a daily process of yielding more and more control to the Holy Spirit and inviting him to fill every part of who we are. This process unfolds one step at a time as we learn to exercise the faith God speaks into our lives.

The reason the early church kept growing and spreading across the Roman Empire with such power was because the living presence of Jesus was replicated in the lives of those who were being discipled in the way of Jesus. This is why the book of Acts is filled with so many references to the Holy Spirit filling, leading, and empowering the followers of Jesus. The Holy Spirit was the one creating Covenantal community among them and fueling the Kingdom power that was flowing through them to transform lives and change human history.

Without an openness to the Holy Spirit and a willingness to yield control to his empowering presence, the movement Jesus began would have faltered and failed in subsequent generations. Because these early Christians were willing to receive the Spirit in faith and give him control of their lives, they were empowered to dramatically multiply Covenantal relationships and exercise miraculous Kingdom authority just as Jesus did.

EMBRACING THE POWER OF THE SPIRIT

The same is true for us today. If we resist the Holy Spirit by holding on to control of our own lives and quench the Spirit by boxing him in with our unbiblical presuppositions, we will not be able to build Covenantal community or exercise Kingdom power the way Jesus did. We need to recognize the world we live in is not a neutral zone. The devil and demons are

> The journey from Covenant identity and obedience to Kingdom authority and power is a daily process of yielding more and more control to the Holy Spirit and inviting him to fill every part of who we are.

not just a theological construction. Powers and principalities are at work in our world, in our churches, and in our lives, actively seeking to prevent God's Kingdom from coming and his will from being done. Jesus had to face the reality of this power before he could begin multiplying disciples and releasing them to do God's will in the world. Certainly we will have to do the same.

The reason our sincere and diligent efforts at reaching new people and helping them to become more like Jesus often fall short is not that we are not trying hard enough. The biggest obstacle we face are powers greater than us working to prevent these things from happening. If we try to take them on alone, we will fail. But if we learn to open ourselves to the power of God's presence within us and operate on the basis of Jesus' authority rather than our own or others', we will discover the power we need to overcome our adversary.

Jesus explained the role of the Holy Spirit: *"But very truly I tell you, it is for your good that I am going away. Unless I go away, the Advocate will not come to you; but if I go, I will send him to you. When he comes, he will prove the world to be in the wrong about sin and righteousness and judgment: about sin, because people do not believe in me; about righteousness, because I am going to the Father, where you can see me no longer; and about judgment, because the prince of this world now stands condemned."* (John 16:7-11)

The Apostle Paul makes the critical distinction between flesh and Spirit in a number of his letters. For Paul, living in the flesh does not simply mean giving into carnal desires—it means all the ways we end up trying to control our lives or the lives of others by our own wisdom and strength. This can include the very things we are trying to do for God, as Paul learned so painfully through his legalistic obsessions and his merciless persecution of Christians.

When Paul talks about operating *in the Spirit*, he is describing the dynamic of yielding control and allowing the Holy Spirit to guide and empower what we say and do. In Galatians 5, Paul uses four different phrases to describe this kind of life: *walk by the Spirit, led by the Spirit, live by the Spirit,* and *keep in step with the Spirit* (Galatians 5:16, 18, 25). It is easy to end up engaging in discipleship and mission in the flesh, but these efforts, no matter how hard we try, will not produce much lasting fruit. The twin biblical themes Jesus modeled for us, Covenant and Kingdom, are so important because they teach us how to walk in the Spirit's wisdom and power rather than our own, producing good fruit that lasts. As always, Jesus sets the example for us to follow.

PUTTING IT ALL TOGETHER

The potent combination of Covenant and Kingdom empowered Jesus to live the extraordinary life he lived and to replicate that life in the lives of others. As we come to recognize these twin themes winding their way through the pages of Scripture, we can begin to draw from the same source of power to live extraordinary lives as well.

In Covenant with his *Father*, Jesus knew his true *identity* from which he determined to obey his Father's will. It was as a part of God's coming Kingdom that Jesus knew his Father to be the *King* of the Universe, and therefore himself as the recipient of divine *authority*. Exercising this authority in submission released God's *power* in Jesus, enabling him to carry out his Father's will completely. As disciples we are called to follow in Jesus' footsteps by the guidance of his indwelling Spirit, learning to find our identity and obedience in Covenant, and claiming the authority and power of God's

Kingdom as he did. We can connect all these dots with this diagram of the life Jesus lived and the life he calls us to imitate:

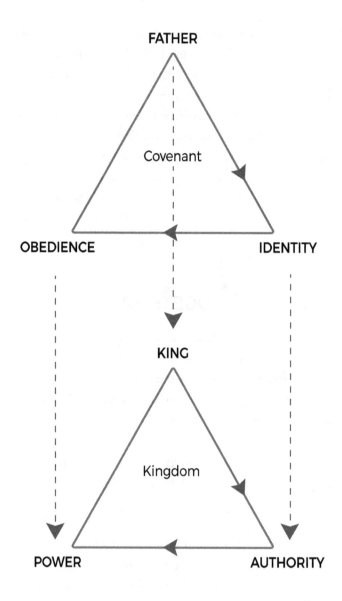

The secret of Jesus' extraordinary life is that he lived simultaneously in both Covenant and Kingdom. By faith in the gracious love of his heavenly Father, Jesus knew himself to be the Son of God (Father → Identity). Realizing his Abba was the King of the Universe (Father → King), Jesus claimed the divine authority that this identity carried (Identity → Authority). Seeking to obey his Father in Covenant faithfulness (Identity → Obedience), Jesus exercised that authority in submission to the Father so God's Kingdom power flowed through him (Authority Power). This power served to accomplish the will of his Father and not just his own (Obedience → Power).

Jesus summed it up on the last night he was with the disciples before going to the cross, explaining the implications for those of us who follow him: *"Do you not believe that I am in the Father and the Father is in me? The words that I say to you I do not speak on my own authority, but the Father who dwells in me does his works. Believe me that I am in the Father and the Father is in me, or else believe on account of the works themselves. Truly, truly, I say to you, whoever believes in me will also do the works that I do; and greater works than these will he do, because I am going to the Father. Whatever you ask in my name, this I will do, that the Father may be glorified in the Son."* (John 14:10-13) Notice the key points he is making about the example he has set for us to follow:

> The potent combination of Covenant and Kingdom empowered Jesus to live the extraordinary life he lived and to replicate that life in the lives of others.

Jesus lived in perfect Covenant union with the Father

(I am in the Father, and the Father is in me)

Jesus spoke on the basis of his Father's authority, not his own

(I do not speak on my own authority)

As a result, the Father's power flowed through Jesus

(the Father who dwells in me does his works)

By faith we can do the same things Jesus did

(whoever believes in me will also do the works that I do)

As we yield control to the Holy Spirit, we can exceed Jesus' results

(greater works than these will he do)

Those who live this kind of life can literally do anything God calls them to do

(Whatever you ask in my name, this I will do, that the Father may be glorified in
the Son)

Jesus is simply explaining the example he has set for us to follow by faith
in the power of his Spirit. The more deeply we trust the Father's adoption
of us as his children, the greater our passion to do his will becomes. The
more fully we recognize our Father as the King of the Universe, the greater
our confidence in the authority Jesus has given us becomes. The more we
step out in faith by claiming that authority to do will of our Father as Jesus
did, the greater power is available for us to do God's will. This is the secret
to living the abundant, transformational, extraordinary life Jesus modeled
for us.

10

STEPPING INTO SPIRITUAL POWER

MY POWER TRIP

I encountered God's power for the first time in my teenage years when I experienced the love of Jesus and he saved me. He changed me. Profoundly. I found a place to stand in God's grace and discovered my identity in him. This gradually transformed everything: my self-image, my confidence, my attitudes, my inner peace, my relationships, and my sense of purpose in life. A desire to do God's will was growing inside of me. By college I had accepted the call into a life of missional leadership. While smuggling Bibles into communist Eastern Europe, I met the amazing woman who was to become my wife.

Driving back to school late one night, I fell asleep at the wheel, drifted into the oncoming lane at 60 miles per hour, and had a head-on collision with a semi-truck traveling the same speed in the opposite direction. Everyone who saw my demolished car agreed that it was an absolute miracle I survived with no more than a shattered right femur and some scratches. Two days later, after back-to-back surgeries, bone grafting, a steel plate, and twenty screws, the best orthopedic surgeons in Seattle told me there was a 50 percent  chance I would lose my leg. Even if it was saved, I would always walk with a limp and would never play sports the way I had. Defying all the doctors' predictions, hundreds of people praying for me resulted in a complete recovery in a matter of months. I knew it was the power of God at work in my life.

As the years unfolded and my faith matured, I continued to experience God's liberating and transforming power in my life and the lives of those I ministered to, primarily through God's Word and the relationships into which he called me. I emerged from seminary and post-graduate studies enthusiastic and confident in what Paul called *"the power of God that brings salvation to everyone who believes"* (Romans 1:16). As a young pastor I saw God's power changing lives by bringing faith, salvation, healing, reconciliation, wisdom, social justice, and even liberation from demonic possession. Witnessing this kind of transformation was exciting, but as time went on, I had to admit it was more the exception than the rule.

Convinced the Bible is not just a collection of religious fables, I wondered why the life of Jesus and his first followers was so much more potent than my life and the lives of those I led. I poured myself into developing more strategic and effective forms of ministry, gathering and training more gifted and committed staff members, always searching for the secret that would lead to a breakthrough where more lives would be transformed than not, but it never seemed to come.

MORE POWER, LORD!

As I mentioned earlier, my eyes were opened in Africa. I spent two weeks in the southeastern part of Uganda, and there I came face to face with the realization that spiritual power is not found in more training, better programs, or more advanced technology. In these humble Ugandan leaders I saw that real, biblical power is manifested in willing hearts yielding by faith to the purpose of God and the empowerment of his Spirit.

During one trip to Uganda I was teaching at an all-day Christian leadership conference under a large blue tarp that provided shade to about a hundred people seated on wooden benches. After an hour of all-out passionate worship and an hour of teaching with a translator, the people launched into another hour of dancing, singing, and clapping to the Lord. Suddenly I heard screams and looked up to see people diving out from under the shade cover. There was a commotion in the middle of the crowd, and then people resumed their places and continued worshiping even more enthusiastically. A few minutes later the exact same thing happened, then the worshipers resumed, and the whole time the musicians never missed a beat.

Curious, I later asked what had happened. They explained that a two-foot long cobra and then a three-foot long cobra appeared in the midst of the worshipers, one after the other, but each time they simply killed it with one of the benches and then resumed worshiping. They told me poisonous snakes are rare in that area and said the local witchdoctor had probably sent the cobras in an effort to disrupt their worship. Apparently it was going to take more than deadly cobras to stop these worshipers! Modern westerners might dismiss this as primitive superstition, but these are people who understand spiritual warfare is real and know how to engage the enemy and win.

That evening I was asked to preach at an open-air evangelistic crusade they had organized in a nearby village. The pastor told me they were praying

God would bring forth a large harvest of new believers through my message. As the sun dipped low on the horizon, I was amazed to see that a crowd about twice the population of the village had gathered to listen. Not feeling much like Billy Graham, it took all my faith to climb on the rickety platform they had erected, so I didn't have much left over to pray for a large evangelistic harvest. After I completed what seemed to me a simple Gospel message, the local pastor who was translating thanked me and asked if anyone wanted to come forward to receive Christ. Cringing, I waited for the uncomfortable silence, followed by the inevitable evangelistic pleading and cajoling. To my surprise there was none of that, because over 200 people immediately came forward, asking to accept Jesus.

In my subsequent experiences with these amazing people, I have seen the same kinds of scenarios played out over and over again. Seeing the incredible fruit of their simple lives, devoid of the many resources I had come to rely on, I realized they had learned to rely on nothing except God's grace and presence in their lives to overcome seemingly impossible obstacles. Trusting their identity in Christ and willing to exercise the authority he has given them, they see God's power flowing through their lives on a regular basis to change the lives of others. These experiences brought me face to face with my own powerlessness and helped me admit to God that I needed more of his transforming power in my life. I came home asking God to help me learn from others how to operate in the power it takes to do his will.

Sometime after returning home, I heard a corroborating testimony that God was indeed powerfully at work in these events I experienced in Uganda. It was a Saturday when the snakes tried to disrupt worship and we saw such a great response to the Gospel. I sent an email to our Teaching Pastor that night and told him what had happened in some detail. That same night a woman in our church who had been close to me and Pam was struggling in her faith. She went to bed plagued with doubts about God's existence. As she lay in bed she prayed, "Lord if you are real, give me a sign to know you are there." During the night she had what seemed a very bizarre dream. She saw me with a large group of people in Uganda. A snake suddenly appeared in the midst of the people and was quickly killed. Then another larger snake appeared, and it too was killed. She woke up thinking it was just a random dream and went to worship at our church the next morning. During the service our Teaching Pastor got up and read the email I had sent him the night before, recounting the story of the snakes. Our friend was overwhelmed by the miraculous way God had answered her cry for help through that strange dream! It has been great to watch God continue to work powerfully in her and her husband's lives since that time.

LEARNING TO EXERCISE AUTHORITY

Jesus regularly exercised spiritual authority in the course of his normal life as an expression of God's Covenant love and a demonstration of God's Kingdom. He spoke prophetically into the lives of his disciples and those he met. He cast demons out of the spiritually oppressed. He healed sick and hurting people everywhere he went. And he trained his disciples to do the same. When Jesus calls us to follow him, he is inviting us to learn a way of life in which God's power flows through us as an expression of his Covenant love and a demonstration of his coming Kingdom.

As we learned more about our identity in Christ and the authority he has given us, we noticed things starting to happen in our church. Certain people who devoted a lot of time to prayer started sensing God speaking to them in ways they had not experienced before. The words and images they received were confirmed by Scripture and the testimony of others. As we studied more about prophecy in the New Testament, we learned how to draw on the mature members of our community to help interpret and apply this growing sense of revelation.

In our smaller and mid-size group gatherings, we began learning how to build one another up, as Paul instructs in 1 Corinthians 14, by intentionally listening to what God might be saying for one another and then speaking these things into each other's lives. We were careful to temper this greater expression of spiritual authority with love and a low-control culture. Our language always reflected how our perception of God's voice is fallible and how the recipient is free to take or leave what we think God might be saying to them. We learned to say, "I think God might be saying..." rather than "Thus says the Lord!" Some of the prophetic images and messages seemed to be for individuals. Others seemed to be for our church as a whole. We found this new experience of God speaking to us through one another exciting, faith building, and incredibly helpful.

Another area where we learned to step into Jesus' power more consistently was physical healing. We had always prayed for the sick and injured to be healed, but now we had a growing sense of God's goodness toward us, our identity in Jesus, and the authority he gives us. We learned that healing ministry is a tangible expression of God's love to those who are hurting. We realized that praying in Jesus' name means exercising the authority he has given us to do the Father's will. We began to pray with greater confidence that a good Father always wants what is good for his children. As we exercised faith in the authority of Jesus, we prayed more boldly, declaring God's intention to heal, and commanding anything standing in the way of that to leave.

The result of this new authority and boldness in prayer was that we started to see more dramatic physical healings than we had ever experienced before. A man's chronic back pain was instantly healed while we prayed for him at the end of a gathering in someone's home. A woman's bound shoulder was suddenly freed, and she recovered a full range of motion while a group laid hands on her and prayed. A woman's cancer diagnosis was reversed overnight. Our teenagers were learning and growing in spiritual authority as well and they began to boldly seek healing for those who were hurting in the youth group. One night they were praying for a high school student who had sprained her ankle in a volleyball match. After they laid hands on her ankle and prayed, they asked if she felt any change. She said no, so they prayed some more. Again no change, so they kept pressing on in prayer. Then she started to feel the pain melt away. She decided to test out her ankle and found she was able to run around the room with no pain. The next day she was back at practice with no injury. There started to be so many testimonies of healing in our community that I could not remember them all anymore! These experiences helped build our faith and confidence in exercising God's power in other areas of our lives.

Along with these more dramatic instances of physical healing, there were numerous testimonies of partial improvement and gradual healing, as well as various forms of emotional and relational healing. Of course, there were also many instances where people we prayed for did not experience any improvement. We came to understand healing ministry as a form of spiritual warfare in which we are fighting to see God's will be done on earth as it is in heaven. When we pray for someone's healing, we are standing with them in a fight against whatever is keeping them from the wholeness God intends for us. When someone does not experience immediate healing, we never blame them for it. We lift them up as a hero for being willing to enter the battle and take ownership for the fact that our community has not yet grown in faith to the point where we can win every battle. But the more we exercised our faith and entered the fight, the more we saw God's power breaking through.

As we learned how to exercise more of the authority Jesus has given us to do the will of our Father, we discovered it was not about esoteric techniques or attention-getting tactics. Jesus' healings and acts of deliverance were always characterized by a noticeable lack of complexity and showmanship. He simply commanded demons to leave, and they left. He declared people healed, and they were. Jesus was incredibly natural in the way he exercised supernatural power and he avoided the limelight. More often than not, he even told those he healed to keep quiet about it.

We learned to step into God's power in the most ordinary ways we could, so it would be clear any extraordinary outcome was God's doing and not due to our special technique or personal charisma. It has become increasingly natural for us to exercise God's supernatural power as he manifests himself in our lives. We are now in the habit of listening for God's voice and expecting him to reveal himself. We are used to simply sharing whatever we receive with others in the hope it will be helpful to them. We don't always see dramatic healings, but as a normal way of life we pray with greater confidence and authority for God's Kingdom to break in and for the enemy to be thwarted. We are learning to live a naturally supernatural way of life as authorized representatives of our King.

A DIFFERENT KIND OF POWER

Why is it so many of us shy away from asking for, or exercising, biblical empowerment? Looking back, I can see three primary reasons I had resisted living more intentionally in God's power. First of all, I was turned off by the style of those who claimed this kind of power. Coming from a long line of Norwegian stock, I have a deep-seated disdain for anything that smacks of self-aggrandizing showmanship and have always been suspicious of those who draw attention to themselves. Based on impressions from television and a few firsthand experiences, I made the false association of spiritual power with this kind of phoniness, manipulation, and pride. As a result I threw the baby out with the bathwater and wanted nothing to do with the exercise of spiritual power. Looking back, I realize how wrong I was. After all, someone hitting you with a golf club is no reason to swear off the game of golf. Or as a wise friend once told me, don't reject a good gift just because you don't like the wrapping paper.

Secondly, I shied away from the exercise of God's power because I didn't want to let go of control. There is comfort in thinking you are in charge of what is going to happen. When you are in control, you can avoid looking foolish and choose things that are comfortable. In our human pride, the enemy deceives us into believing that we can do what we are meant to do by our own strength. Nothing could be further from the truth. As we saw earlier, this is what Paul calls living in the flesh. When we operate by our own wisdom and power in the flesh, we actually make ourselves susceptible to powers greater than ourselves and jeopardize the most important things in our lives. Paul says the results of living in the flesh are things like *"sexual immorality, impurity and debauchery; idolatry and witchcraft; hatred, discord, jealousy, fits of rage, selfish ambition, dissensions, factions and envy; drunkenness, orgies, and the like"* (Galatians 5:19-21). This is what we risk when we keep holding onto control instead of yielding to the Spirit's power!

Thirdly, I resisted the Spirit's power in my life and ministry because I was afraid. In spite of the many positive ways I had experienced God's transforming power in my life, I somehow got the message that power was intrinsically bad. This came in part from hearing about notorious abuses of spiritual power, but even more so from a church culture that was suspicious of anyone claiming this kind of authority. Institutions are born out of a need to protect dynamic movements from the misuse of power. We all need accountability; however, often we go too far by developing structures that are hostile toward even a healthy exercise of authority and power. These kinds of institutional cultures produce managers rather than leaders and reward maintenance rather than mission. In this kind of environment, I assumed it was wrong to claim authority and was afraid that exercising spiritual power would lead to something bad.

The Bible makes it absolutely clear that God's power is intrinsically good. When God exercised his infinite power to create the Universe he deemed the result very good (Genesis 1:31). God used that same power to overcome Pharaoh and free the people of Israel from slavery. That same power overcame the grave when Jesus rose from the dead. By that same power Jesus has promised to return, overthrow all the forces of evil on earth, and renew all of creation, once and for all establishing his eternal Kingdom. From the Old Testament to the New, we see God's power is a power for good and not for evil, that God is always for us and never against us, and that his power alone can free people from sin, death, hell, and the devil.

I am happy to say that I have overcome much of my resistance to exercising Jesus' authority in expressing his Covenant love and demonstrating his Kingdom power because it has become a source of blessing and joy in my life. A brief story will illustrate what I mean: A few years ago a woman named Cindy came to one of our 3DM Learning Community gatherings in San Francisco. She suffered from a combination of Lupus and Myasthenia Gravis, which caused her constant pain and significantly reduced her mobility. We prayed for Cindy to be healed, but when she returned six months later she was walking with a cane and her condition had worsened. We prayed for her again, but six months later when she returned her condition was still worse. In spite of our prayers, by the final training session she was in even greater pain and confined to a wheelchair. We prayed for God to heal her with all the faith and love we had, said our goodbyes, and hoped something would change.

It was nearly two years later when we saw Cindy again at a 3DM event. She was so dramatically improved I didn't even recognize her for the first day. When we realized who she was and asked her what had happened, she told us that during the final prayer session two years earlier something changed. Her pain started to diminish and her muscle control began to return. The next day she was even better. She stopped taking all her medications and continued to improve steadily until, before long, she was walking normally again. She returned to her doctors and they told her the Lupus and Myasthenia Gravis was completely gone. Today there is no sign of her disease and she walks four miles in an hour every day. Cindy has been miraculously healed!

When Cindy told us her story we were amazed at God's goodness and power. I was teaching later that day on learning to live a more naturally supernatural life, so I asked her to tell her story during that session and she agreed. For background to what happened next I need to explain I have two collapsed disks in my lower back that have caused me constant pain for the past eight years. I have sought every imaginable kind of treatment during that time and nothing has given me any lasting relief. A year ago I inquired with a specialist about surgery to end my pain, but the surgeon told me an operation would only cause more long-term problems. For the last five years I have asked for prayer at every opportunity, but with no apparent effect. To be honest, I was so tired of it all that I had stopped asking for prayer.

As Cindy began to tell her story of healing that day, I felt a strange tingling in my lower back and radiating down my legs. At first I thought it was a spike of nerve pain that so regularly plagued me, but then I realized it felt good. Then I wondered if I was having an emotional reaction to Cindy's testimony, but I could feel it was much stronger than goosebumps. Finally I began to wonder if God was doing something through Cindy's story. By the end of the day I realized that I had no pain in my lower back for the first time in eight years. At first I was cautious to claim healing for fear the pain would return, but since that day I have had no pain to speak of in my lower back! I can feel that there is still something wrong in my lower back, but it is no longer causing me pain. I still don't understand exactly what happened, but somehow just hearing Cindy's testimony finally broke through whatever was standing in the way of the healing I had sought for so long. Maybe it is what Paul wrote to the Romans long ago, *"So faith comes from hearing, and hearing through the word of Christ."* (Romans 10:17)

About six months after this book was first published, I was in Calgary leading a training event when one of the participants approached me, thanking me for writing about my healing. He told me that his wife Sheila had suffered for three years with severe lower back pain, similar to mine. Like me, no treatments or prayer seemed to alleviate her constant pain. One night she was reading my explanation of spiritual power when she came to the story of Cindy's and my healings which you have just read. As she was reading, she felt a tingling in her lower back and all the pain melted away! To this day she is freed of that constant back pain. Once again, the power of testimony ignited the faith that was needed to bring the breakthrough for healing.

God's power is always an expression of his love. He has the power to protect us. He has the power to provide for us. He has the power to set us free. Even when God uses his power to discipline us, it is always out of love. Paul captures the intrinsic connection between God's power and his love in this prayer for the Ephesians: *"I pray that out of his glorious riches he may strengthen you with power through his Spirit in your inner being, so that Christ may dwell in your hearts through faith. And I pray that you, being rooted and established in love, may have power, together with all the Lord's people, to grasp how wide and long and high and deep is the love of Christ, and to know this love that surpasses knowledge—that you may be filled to the measure of all the fullness of God. Now to him who is able to do immeasurably more than all we ask or imagine, according to his power that is at work within us, to him be glory in the church and in Christ Jesus throughout all generations, for ever and ever! Amen."* (Ephesians 3:16-21) Why would we ever resist that kind of power?

THE IMMEASURABLE GREATNESS OF HIS POWER

We have seen that Jesus was deeply rooted in his identity as the Father's Son. Because his Father is the King of the Universe, Jesus knew his identity brought great authority. He claimed this authority, and so God's power flowed through Jesus to accomplish the Father's will on earth as it is in heaven. Jesus passed on both his identity and authority to those who followed him. They began to do the same kinds of things he had done. Jesus' Kingdom has continued for 2,000 years to the extent his followers have learned to operate in the same life-changing biblical power he did. The agents of his Kingdom in the centuries to come will be those who know who they really are in Jesus, and who are willing to claim the authority he has given us.

Many of us have not realized Jesus' power is for us to exercise. But Jesus made it clear—the authority which gives us the power to do God's will in Jesus' name is not a special privilege bestowed exclusively on pastors, prophets, or the spiritually elite. One day the disciples saw someone they did not even know driving out demons in Jesus' name. When they complained to Jesus, he said, *"Do not stop him. No one who does a miracle in my name can in the next moment say anything bad about me, for whoever is not against us is for us."* (Mark 9:39-40) You don't need a title or a position to be a conduit of God's transforming Kingdom. You don't even need to be known to the recognized leaders of the church. Every person who genuinely accepts the name of Jesus in Covenant receives the authority to exercise the power of God's Kingdom on his behalf.

Some doubt that the power Jesus exercised is still operative today. But this transformational empowerment did not end when Jesus ascended into heaven. Rather, it became the norm for the followers of Jesus over the next three centuries. On the day of Pentecost, the Holy Spirit was poured out on all the disciples, and they went on to teach with the same authority and power Jesus did, and to heal and cast out demons in his name as well (Acts 5:12-16). This was not restricted to the holy city—under the pressure of persecution, it soon began to spread beyond the walls of Jerusalem into surrounding Judea, neighboring Samaria, and then into the wider world beyond, just as Jesus predicted (Acts 1:8; Acts 8-12). It wasn't long until Paul and his disciples were taking this movement to the far reaches of the Roman Empire.

The startling spread of early Christianity against all odds begins to make sense when we realize Jesus passed on to his followers, and they to theirs, what Paul calls *"the immeasurable greatness of his power toward us who believe"* (Ephesians 1:19). It's not that these followers of Jesus floated through history immune to the power of evil in the world. On the contrary, they were caught up

> Jesus' Kingdom has continued for 2,000 years to the extent his followers have learned to operate in the same life-changing biblical power he did. The agents of his Kingdom in the centuries to come will be those who know who they really are in Jesus, and who are willing to claim the authority he has given us.

in the midst of a cosmic, spiritual battle that continues until Jesus' return and final victory.

Writing in the second century AD, the apologist Tertullian testifies to the authority and power typical of these early disciples when he writes, *"Torment, rack, condemn, crush us. For your injustice is the proof of our innocence. God permits us to suffer these things for that very purpose... Yet the most exquisite cruelty, which you can devise, avails you nothing, but rather induces the more to become Christians. As often as we are cut down by your persecutions, we spring up the more abundantly: the blood of Christians is the seed of the faith."*[14]

It wasn't until Constantine managed to usurp the authority of Jesus, institutionalize it in the structures of the church, and substitute the power of the state for God's power that the dramatic movement of early Christianity was robbed of its revolutionary momentum. Gradually, the leaders of this movement who had learned to operate in Jesus' name at all costs increasingly began acting instead in the name of a state-run institution that provided them with physical comforts and social status. Increasingly, Christianity was reduced to a set of agreed-upon doctrines, while faithfulness was defined by adherence to these teachings and participation in the rituals of the institution.

No longer tested by the challenges of a pagan world hostile to their faith, the followers of Jesus forfeited their authority and power. Roman patrons turned them into clients, European lords turned them into serfs, and now capitalistic culture has turned many into religious consumers. We have largely forgotten how to claim the authority of Jesus and follow his example of exercising God's power on behalf of the faithless, broken, and oppressed. We are the inheritors of this spiritual amnesia, and now face a

---

14. Quintus Septimius Florens Tertullian, *Apology*, trans. Temple Chevallier, 2nd edition, (London: Rivington , 1851), chapter 50, section 361.

postmodern, pagan challenge threatening to consign the movement of Jesus to irrelevance and impotence. The time has come to awaken, shake off our forgetfulness, and recapture the movement of empowered missional disciples who are once again following Jesus and carrying out the mission of God in his authority and power.

OUR MARCHING ORDERS

When Jesus gave us our final marching orders to continue doing what he did, he prefaced it by saying, *"All authority in heaven and on earth has been given to me"* (Matthew 28:18). The resurrection of Jesus made indisputably clear what his life of love and power had already demonstrated—that there is no higher authority anywhere. The earliest Christian creed says: *"Therefore God has highly exalted him and bestowed on him the name that is above every name, so that at the name of Jesus every knee should bow, in heaven and on earth and under the earth, and every tongue confess*

> The time has come to awaken, shake off our forgetfulness, and recapture the movement of empowered missional disciples who are once again following Jesus and carrying out the mission of God in his authority and power.

that Jesus Christ is Lord, to the glory of God the Father." (Philippians 2:9-11) The point is clear: if Jesus has the power to conquer death itself, then nothing is beyond his reach.

With the word therefore, Jesus transferred his ultimate authority to those of us who answer the call to follow his example: *"Go therefore and make disciples of all nations, baptizing them in the name of the Father and of the Son and of the Holy Spirit, teaching them to observe all that I have commanded you. And behold, I am with you always, to the end of the age."* (Matthew 28:19-20) Jesus transfers the authority we need in order to gain access to the power it takes to make disciples who can do the things Jesus did and carry on his revolutionary movement.

First Jesus points to the act of baptism in the name of the Triune God—a powerful expression of Covenant in which God speaks our true identity over us and pours out his Holy Spirit upon us. Then Jesus calls us to empower our followers to live out the Kingdom by teaching them how to do the very things Jesus taught us to do. His point is clear: our Great Commission to make disciples who can do everything Jesus did is rooted in the biblical empowerment of Covenant and Kingdom.

VIVA LA REVOLUCION!

On July 14, 1789 the people of Paris stormed the fortified Bastille Prison, a hated symbol of the arbitrary and oppressive rule of a long-outdated feudalism. By day's end the crowd had taken control of the prison along with 30,000 pounds of gunpowder and 30,000 muskets. The young French King, Louis XVI, is reported to have asked an advisor, "Is it a rebellion?" "No sire," the advisor reputedly replied, "It is a revolution!" In less than three weeks, feudalism was officially abolished in France, and by summer's end the "Declaration of the Rights of Man and of the Citizen" was proclaimed law. The French Revolution was officially underway, marking the end of one era and the beginning of the next.

Jesus was, without a doubt, the greatest revolutionary this world has ever seen. He was not interested in the coercive tactics or violent methodologies of the nationalistic rebels of his day (Matthew 26:55). Instead he focused on the revolutionary biblical DNA of Covenant and Kingdom, carried out in these three key dimensions:

BIBLICAL EMPOWERMENT UP

DISCIPLING CULTURE IN

MISSIONAL COMMUNITY OUT

When Jesus turned over tables in the Temple courts, he announced an end to the spiritual feudalism imposed by both Sadducees and Pharisees on the ordinary people. When the risen Jesus breathed the Spirit on his disciples and commissioned them to make disciples and carry out the mission he had begun, the revolution was officially underway. This rapidly expanding revolutionary movement exhibited more power than the Bastille's 30,000 pounds of gunpowder could ever hope to muster! This too was the end of one era and the beginning of the next.

In our day, the holdovers of spiritual feudalism have combined forces with the current regime of modern consumerism and have locked away spiritual power behind the twin walls of clerical elitism and consumeristic entitlement. The signs of rebellion are all around, as a restive laity sense they were created for so much more but don't quite know how to claim it. Rebel leaders abound, emerging with a promise to storm the gates of traditionalism and return this power to the people, yet they offer no proven blueprint for what to do with it once this power is seized. Like the excesses of the French Revolution, these rebellious outbursts inevitably result in lots of blood, but little lasting or productive value.

What we need is a truly revolutionary leader with the genetic code required to build the new world that lies ahead. Jesus is, of course, this leader. The New Covenant he established in his blood and the transforming Kingdom he demonstrated by God's power create the DNA of the new world into which we are called. By his authority we have been given the naturally supernatural power it will take to build that new reality. In the remaining two parts of this book, we will explore how this biblical DNA is the basis of building a truly discipling culture that multiplies missional communities of ordinary people who are empowered to bring this revolutionary Good News of the Kingdom to the world.

The missional pioneers of postmodern Europe have begun to blaze the trail for us in North America by recapturing Jesus' DNA for today and developing the transferable tools we need to learn once again how to make disciples and release them for mission in Jesus' name. For over twenty years, these European rebels have been leading revolutionary change at an evolutionary pace so others can join in the movement. It has been 1,700 years since Constantine and Roman culture reshaped the Christian movement after its own design. It now falls to us to restore a Jesus-shaped movement for our time. Come and join us in this revolution of love and grace!

PART 2

JESUS-SHAPED DISCIPLESHIP

11

FROM CONSUMERS TO PRODUCERS

CONSUMER CONDITIONING

When Pam and I were smuggling Bibles behind the Iron Curtain in the mid-1980s, we were always struck by the stark contrasts between the capitalist West and the communist East. Under communism the depressingly grey and colorless atmosphere of public spaces were designed by bureaucrats focused on function to the exclusion of form. Infrastructure and technology always seemed about two decades out of date. The population trying to navigate this totalitarian system was marked by anxious glances and down-turned eyes. But the difference that stood out above all the rest was the complete lack of product selection. Row after row of high rise apartments, each one identical to the next; lines of flimsy cars, all the same make and model, winding through the streets; rows of half-empty grocery shelves, offering no more than one brand of any type of food.

One time our team was covertly delivering books to Christian leaders in

Pilsen, Czechoslovakia. Before going out to meet our contacts, we sat down for dinner in the faded elegance of an old French restaurant. The linen tablecloths and real silver gave us hope for a decent meal. The tuxedo-clad waiter handed each of us a large, leather-bound menu and then returned to take our order. I decided on the Chicken Cordon Bleu. The waiter apologized, saying they were out of Cordon Bleu. Scanning the menu, I asked for the Boeuf Bourguignon, and again the waiter apologized. So I asked if they had the Confit de Canard, but the waiter simply shook his head. Exasperated I asked, "What do you have?" and the waiter sheepishly pointed on the menu to the Coq au Vin. We said, "OK, we'll have five orders of the Coq au Vin!"

In the competitive culture of western capitalism, no restaurant could survive by carrying only one dish on its menu, nor a grocery store with only one brand nor an auto manufacturer with only one model. The genius that drives capitalistic societies to produce a better product at a cheaper price is the competition that multiple brands produce. We walk in our grocery stores and expect a nearly endless supply of product selection. We look at the eight types of BBQ sauce on the shelf and quickly compare cost, quantity, quality, and style. What is the price per ounce? Do I want Kansas City smoky flavor, Memphis-style vine-gar-based, or Carolina mustard sauce? Is the bottle attractive and functional? Is it on sale? Our brains are conditioned for this kind of comparison shopping, and we expect manufacturers and retailers to cater to our every whim in order to earn our business.

But something even more powerful than brand competition drives our western economies. From our earliest years, the culture we live in promotes consumption as a primal activity. Annual traditions such as Christmas and birthdays are centered on the ritual of unwrapping gifts, which are of-ten framed as an affirmation of our worth as individuals and an assurance of our place in the family. Children's television programming is laced with advertising designed to shape our brand consciousness from an early age. It does not take long for our sense of identity to be shaped by what we acquire. By middle school we wear t-shirts that advertise our favorite brands, plaster stickers on our notebooks emblazoned with popular logos, and claim we will die if our parents don't buy us a certain brand of shoes or jeans.

This pattern is reinforced as we move into adulthood and begin earning an income that allows us to make significant purchases and promotes shopping as a way of life. Recent research has demonstrated impulse purchases are directly related to the levels of the chemical dopamine in our brain, which produces a temporary feeling of well-being. On top of these cultural and chemical factors, the social expectations that drive consumerism are huge. We are constantly expected to upgrade our clothing, our technology, and our activities to whatever is currently in vogue. The nature of a capitalistic society requires its citizens to keep purchasing products if its economy is to keep growing. We have seen the catastrophic impact on our national economic health when people stop spending due to fear of threats, like the terrorist attacks of September 11, 2001. When the President of the United States goes on national television and implores people to resume spending, we get the message that consuming is our patriotic duty.

CHURCH SHOPPING

Given the nature of western society, is it any wonder that modern churches have, sometimes unwittingly, adopted a consumeristic culture? We take it for granted when a Christian family moves into a new neighborhood they will naturally begin shopping for a new church. By this we mean they will visit a variety of churches and compare the quality of what each has to offer. How are the facilities? What times are the services? Do they have programs my kids will enjoy? Is the music up to my standards and according to my taste? Does the preacher capture my attention and keep my interest?

Because we take consumerism for granted, we assume the answers to these questions will determine what church this new family will choose to join.

Church leaders are painfully aware of these consumeristic realities. Because we know most people will choose their church based on how well it meets their perceived needs and preferences, most of us work hard to provide what people want, within the limits of our own values and convictions. We build facilities that are attractive and comfortable. We design programs that are relevant and value-added. We offer services that meet or exceed people's expectations. We advertise through direct mail and try to motivate our members to invite their friends. We do this all in the hope that we will attract them to participate in our church, so they will encounter God's love in Jesus, be changed, and in turn change the world. Our ultimate goal is often good, but the means by which we seek that goal is inevitably shaped by our consumeristic culture.

All churches are subject to the pressure of consumerism. It doesn't matter if you are leading a church of thousands with multiple campuses, or are planting a new church in your living room. The nagging question is always in the back our mind: "What will get people to come?" This question might be driven by the pressure to balance a multimillion-dollar budget, the commitment to preserve your friends' jobs, or just the dread of being labeled as someone whose church plant failed. In a competitive, consumeristic culture, we know attracting customers and selling our goods and services is the key to survival. Of course we would never use this language in our mission statement or strategy sessions, but that is exactly what is going on.

Over 50 years ago, in his classic book, *Understanding Media*, Marshall McLuhan coined the now-famous phrase "the medium is the message."[15]

---

15. Marshall McLuhan, *Understanding Media: The Extensions of Man* (New York: McGraw Hill, 1964), p. 1.

He was pointing out that it is not only the things we express, but also the way we express them, that affect change. This is not a value judgment—it is simply an observable fact. When cultures of oral tradition gave way to reading the written word, it changed the way people experienced stories. A story was no longer primarily a corporate experience, but increasingly an individual one. When time was no longer measured by the angle of the sun but by mechanical devices that counted out minutes and seconds, it changed the way people structured their daily life. On time took on an entirely different meaning. McLuhan's point was not that this is necessarily a bad thing, but simply that we usually don't notice this dynamic and so are not prepared for its consequences.

We can see this same dynamic at work in the western church today. In an increasingly secularized society where participation in religious institutions continues to decline, there is growing pressure to attract more participants. This pressure has resulted in all kinds of innovative approaches to the media of our ministries. Some have built multimillion-dollar theater-style auditoriums with cutting-edge video systems where we use coordinated advertising campaigns to promote our culturally relevant series of highly practical messages. Others have transformed traditional spaces into intentionally relational environments with couches and café tables lit by a constellation of candles to highlight an ancient-urban vibe meant to appeal to the latest hipster impulse. Still others of us have stripped away all the frills to reveal a simple, organic church seemingly devoid of distractions or obstacles.

It doesn't matter if you are leading a church of thousands with multiple campuses, or are planting a new church in your living room. The nagging question is always in the back our mind: "What will get people to come?"

The point is not which one is right or better. The point is to recognize the unintended message the media of our ministry is communicating. As long as we are driven by the goal of attracting more participants to our community, the means by which we seek to achieve this goal will inevitably communicate the message of consumerism. For 25 years I led churches with the clear purpose of helping people meet Jesus, be changed by his grace and love, and be empowered to do his will in the world. In order to meet that goal, we created many types of media (buildings, technology, staff positions, programs, teaching series, events, etc.) designed to reach new people and increase the positive effect of our mission. What I did not realize was how significantly the way we were carrying out our mission was shaping the nature of what that mission was producing. We wanted to make disciples who would be empowered to fulfill God's mission, but too often we ended up with consumeristic Christians who expected the church staff to meet their needs and who resisted the call to take the risk of spiritual leadership. We were teaching one thing, but our media was teaching another.

JESUS' MISSIONAL MEDIA

How are we supposed to reach more people with the Good News of Jesus in our competitive culture without unintentionally reinforcing the ubiquitous message of consumerism? As always we would be wise to look carefully at the person and life of Jesus, asking ourselves how he carried out his mission. Immediately after describing Jesus' dramatic baptism in the Jordan River, John tells us Jesus invited Andrew and Simon to *"come and see"* and they spent the day with him (John 1:39). The next day Jesus said to Philip, *"Follow me,"* and Philip brought along his friend Nathaniel (John 1:43-46). By the third day, at least five of them went with Jesus to a wedding in Cana, and that's when things really started to get interesting. By the time Jesus had left his hometown of Nazareth and established a new home in Capernaum, he had gathered an extended family of followers from whom he chose twelve to be his closest disciples. This core comprised the *"living stones"* with which Jesus was beginning to build his church.

As we read the Gospels carefully, we see that the media of Jesus' mission was discipleship. Not necessarily discipleship as we have typically defined it, but discipleship as a transformational relationship and an empowering way of life. Jesus invited people into his life, giving them full access to everything that was his. He invested his truth and life in them, trained them to live the way he did, and then released them with the authority and power they needed to go and do the same with others. He made it clear that this way of discipleship was both life-giving and costly. He told his followers the yoke of his discipleship was light and easy, but also warned them that if they chose to follow him, they would need to take up a cross and lay down their lives. This was a profoundly anti-consumeristic way to carry out his mission.

Alan Hirsch points out that discipleship and consumerism are mutually exclusive: *"We can't seem to make disciples based on a consumerist approach to the faith. We plainly cannot consume our way into discipleship. All of us must become much more active in the equation of becoming life-long followers of Jesus. Consumption is detrimental to discipleship."*[16] When we recognize consumerism is counterproductive to discipleship, it leads to some challenging conclusions about the way we are seeking to fulfill our mission. What are we willing to stop doing that feeds a consumer culture? What cost are we willing to pay to begin developing a discipling culture?

Some will point out that Jesus attracted large crowds of people everywhere he went, and of course that is true. But attracting large crowds was not the primary means of Jesus' mission, nor did he call his followers to seek after such large gatherings. The crowds were a byproduct of the extraordinary character and fruitfulness of Jesus' mission. The authority of his teaching, his ability to heal any disease, and his absolute power over evil was a strong draw to the disaffected, the hurting, and the curious. Consumerism is not a solely modern phenomenon; as long as people have been curved in upon themselves, there has always been the propensity to ask, "What's in it for me?" But Jesus consistently inoculated the crowds against consumerism by

16. Hirsch, Alan, *The Forgotten Ways: Reactivating the Missional Church* (Grand Rapids, Brazos, 2006), p. 45.

directly confronting a self-serving orientation. To the crowds that sought him after his miraculous feeding of the five thousand, Jesus said, *"Truly, truly, I say to you, you are seeking me, not because you saw signs, but because you ate your fill of the loaves."* (John 6:26)

Instead of recognizing this mistake and turning their attention to the substance of Jesus' teaching and example, they asked him, *"Then what sign do you do, that we may see and believe you? What work do you perform?"* (John 6:30). Talk about missing the point! One of the problems in dealing with people in a large group is that it allows for very little personal accountability. A mob mentality feeds the human tendency to seek reward without responsibility. Jesus saw the consumerism of this crowd was only going to get worse, so he steadily increased the challenge of his teaching, telling the crowd eternal life was found by eating (literally: "munching") his flesh and drinking his blood (John 6:54). By the time he finished, most of the crowd had disappeared, along with some who had considered themselves his disciples. Only the core group remained.

Why did Jesus intentionally sharpen the edge of this scandalous teaching until the crowd of eager seekers had disbursed? Because he knew the media is the message. He understood that if his movement was defined by large crowds attracted to impressive displays of power and free lunches, self-indulgence would become the message. Instead, Jesus made it clear that his followers were to be producers, not consumers. He described us as branches who abide in the vine and produce good fruit that lasts. Unfruitful branches get broken off and thrown into the fire (John 15:1-5). Jesus chose to prune the consumeristic crowd back to a nub of twelve disciples and an extended family of followers, because this is the best context to live out the message of Jesus and multiply

> As we read the Gospels carefully, we see that the media of Jesus' mission was discipleship. Not necessarily discipleship as we have typically defined it, but discipleship as a transformational relationship and an empowering way of life.

that way of life in the lives of others. With this family of disciples Jesus laid the foundations of a movement that would alter the course of human history. In 2,000 years nothing has changed. Jesus is still calling us to become producers by learning how to make disciples and live as members of his extended family. Let's take a closer look at what that entails.

12

LEARNING TO FOLLOW JESUS

FIRST-CENTURY RABBIS AND DISCIPLES

I had the privilege of studying New Testament archaeology in Jerusalem for a year and I have led people on unique pilgrimages to the Holy Land in "The Footsteps of Jesus" with Pam for more than twenty years now. One of the things I enjoy when we introduce ancient biblical sites to new people is pointing out the way artifacts from the past often get reused for different purposes in the present.

For instance, in Capernaum there is a huge millstone from the first century, once used to grind grain, but now serving the monks there as a planter. In Jerusalem there is a Roman sarcophagus (stone coffin) reused as the basin of a medieval fountain. This is a picture of what often happens with biblical discipleship. Since most of us do not live in a culture with disciples and rabbis, it is easy to misunderstand the nature of biblical discipleship. At first glance we naturally assume that huge stone was designed for planting flowers, when actually it was meant to crush olives for oil. It takes some experience to distinguish a coffin from a fountain basin, but it can be learned quite easily if we have someone to point it out. If we are going to learn to live the life Jesus modeled for us, we are going to have to take a closer look at this ancient cultural artifact called discipleship and discover how it actually worked in Jesus' time so we don't accidently confuse its intended purpose.

In first-century Jewish society, the most important person in the community was the rabbi. He was the interpreter of the Bible, leader of the synagogue, arbiter of legal disputes, and cornerstone of the educational system. When children were about five years old, they would go to the synagogue to attend *Beth Sefer*, "the house of the book." The rabbi would teach them to read and write and memorize the first five books of the Old Testament. Around age ten, most of these children would return home to start learning a trade or preparing for marriage. But the rabbi would choose the most promising students to continue their education in *Beth Midrash*, "the house of interpretation." They would read and discuss the rest of the Old Testament books, along with the oral tradition of rabbinical interpretation, debating various applications of the scriptures. By the age of fifteen, these students would also return home to begin working in the family business and preparing to start a family of their own.

In *Beth Midrash* the rabbi would observe his students closely, looking for the standouts—those unique individuals whom he believed had the potential, not only to know what he knew, but learn how to do what he did, and ultimately become the kind of person he was. The rabbi accepted these few exceptional students as his *talmidim*, a Hebrew word we usually translate disciples. *Talmidim* went everywhere the rabbi went, ate what the rabbi ate, and slept where the rabbi slept. They hung on his every word, watched his every step, and were ready to jump in whenever the rabbi asked them to join him in what he was doing. The point of discipleship in first-century Judaism was to live in such a close relationship with the rabbi that by fol-

lowing his example you could learn to do what he did and so become like him. I love the ancient rabbinical blessing based on a passage from the Mishnah, "Follow your rabbi, drink in his words, and be covered by the dust of his feet."[17]

When Jesus was walking along the shore of the Sea of Galilee and said to the fishermen busy at their work, *"Come follow me,"* he was inviting them to become *talmidim.* We expect them to answer, "Where are you going? How long will we be gone? What's in it for me?" Instead, as Mark records, *"At once they left their nets and followed him."* (Mark 1:18) Until we understand the nature of discipleship, we are puzzled by this immediate and absolute response of the fishermen to Jesus' invitation.

Becoming a talmid was one of the highest honors someone could attain in first-century Jewish society. It must have been shocking for these fishermen to receive this invitation from Jesus. After all, these were students who hadn't made the grade. They left the synagogue school to learn a trade because they weren't considered good enough to become disciples. Now this amazing rabbi, Jesus of Nazareth, was inviting them to become his disciples. It would be like steel workers in Pennsylvania receiving a full scholarship from Harvard Medical School and then being invited to become roommates with their favorite professor. No wonder they dropped

17. Jacob Neusner, editor, *The Mishnah: A New Translation* (New Haven: Yale University, 1988), Avot 1:4.

their nets and followed Jesus!

Jesus went on to invite twelve very unlikely men to be his *talmidim* as part of his extended family. For the next three years, Jesus invested in these disciples, sharing his whole life with them in Covenant relationship. During this time Jesus showed them how to live out God's Kingdom, inviting them to participate with him and then sending them out to do what he did on their own. Jesus' goal was for them to be able to do everything he did by the same authority and power he had received. He said it this way: *"A disciple is not above his teacher, but everyone when he is fully trained will be like his teacher."* (Luke 6:40) Disciples do not just learn to know what their rabbi knows, but also to do what their rabbi does and so become like the rabbi.

IMITATION OR INNOVATION?

In the modern western world, following a rabbi and learning to do what he or she does is a foreign concept. To most of us, imitation is usually a bad word. Think of saccharin, Rolex knockoffs, and Milli Vanilli. In a culture where individuality is lifted up as the ideal, imitating others is disparaged and discouraged. We drum it into our children from their earliest days that they are unique and special, like no one else on the planet. This is most certainly true—each is a precious child of God created in his image—but in an individualistic culture this can be taken to mean our value is somehow rooted in our independence from others. Asking for help becomes weakness. Looking to role models becomes a lack of creativity. Like those rugged individualists who crossed the plains and pioneered the West before us, we are left to face and overcome the challenges of life on our own.

But every accomplished jazz musician will tell you that improvisational greatness is preceded by countless hours of playing scales and copying the techniques of those who have gone before them. The great Renaissance masters were able to break new ground because they had first learned to paint by joining the school of an established master and replicating their work. An individualistic culture that craves instant gratification sells us the lie that we can achieve excellence by beginning with solitary innovation. The truth is that real, creative achievement comes when imitation precedes innovation. Those who submit to the discipline of learning from the example of others with more experience are the ones who are able to surpass their teachers and pioneer new territory.

SO WHO ARE YOU IMITATING?

It has been clear to me my entire Christian life that discipleship is central to Jesus and therefore is of great importance to those who claim his name. It's hard to read the Great Commission and come to any other conclusion! But in my individualistic world, discipleship was always defined as the solitary pursuit of information. It meant having a daily quiet time by myself where I read the Bible silently and reflected on it internally. It meant spending time alone in prayer. It meant learning to practice spiritual disciplines by reading books about fasting and meditation and solitude. I assumed that acquiring more biblical knowledge, theological insight, and spiritual practices would change me and make me more like Jesus. Imitating someone who is helping me learn how to follow Jesus never occurred to me.

Obviously spending time alone with God in the Word, prayer, and study are incredibly important things. Jesus spent time alone with the Father, and we are called to the same. However, simply seeking more information is not enough. Solitary spiritual practices are not enough. Discipleship is not something we can read from a book (including this one!) and figure out on our own. Biblical discipleship is intrinsically relational because it is an invitation into a mentoring relationship. A person can only be called a disciple in relationship to his or her rabbi. Gaining revelatory information from God is critical, but we also need a real life example to imitate.

Jesus' disciples had the opportunity, not only to hear everything Jesus said, but also to watch everything he did. The information they received through Jesus' profound teaching was matched by the powerful example he set for them as he welcomed the outcast, fed the hungry, healed the broken, delivered the possessed, and raised the dead (Luke 7-8). Before long they had the opportunity to participate in the very things Jesus was doing. The disciples watched as Jesus blessed and broke the bread, but then Jesus asked them to distribute the five loaves and two fish as it miraculously multiplied to feed the multitudes (Luke 9:16-17). They learned to do the things Jesus did by actually imitating his way of life. As they grew in their competency, Jesus sent them out with his authority to do what they had seen him do. They reported back to Jesus with great joy that, in his name, they were able to do the same things he did (Luke 10:17). After three years they were fully trained, and Jesus commissioned them to go out into every part of the world (Acts 1:8). As they went out into new places, they did with others everything Jesus had done with them, but each in their own unique way.

As the disciples of Jesus began to multiply, they continued to follow the same pattern Jesus had set for them, inviting others to follow their example as they were following Jesus' example. When writing to his disciples in Corinth, Paul said it simply: *"Be imitators of me, as I am of Christ."* (1 Corinthians 11:1) Paul was very clear that he was an imperfect example, but he also knew Jesus was present and alive in him through the power of his Spirit. This indwelling Jesus is who Paul was inviting his followers to imitate. As important as it is to read about Jesus in the New Testament, and as much as his Spirit is present to transform and empower us, we all need a real-life example of Jesus to follow. Paul shows us that Jesus-shaped discipleship begins with Information, gets put into practice through Imitation, and is ultimately released in a life of fruitful Innovation.

> Discipleship is not something we can read from a book (including this one!) and figure out on our own. Biblical discipleship is intrinsically relational because it is an invitation into a mentoring relationship.

When we put this on the template of Jesus' three-dimensional life, it looks like this:

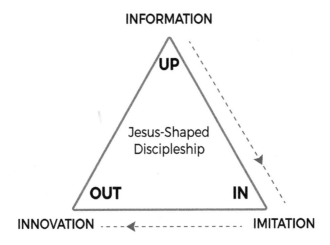

Jesus-shaped discipleship begins with revelatory information from God (UP), and is combined with relational proximity where practical demonstration can be imitated (IN). Once trained this way, rabbis then release their disciples to innovatively fulfill their own unique calling as they raise up another generation of disciples (OUT). This is what we mean when we talk about discipleship. We can learn how to move from information to imitation and achieve fruitful innovation by looking more closely at the specific way Jesus interacted with his disciples.

JESUS' METHOD OF DISCIPLESHIP

Just before Jesus began calling people to follow him, he launched his ministry by describing the heart of his discipling process: *"The time is fulfilled, and the kingdom of God is at hand; repent and believe in the gospel"* (Mark 1:15). The term we translate *time* here is the Greek word *kairos*, which is quite different from the linear, chronological passage of time. *Kairos* refers to a critical moment in time, a crossroads where God opens up an opportunity to us, and we are called to choose which way we will go. The

> Paul shows us that Jesus-shaped discipleship begins with Information, gets put into practice through Imitation, and is ultimately released in a life of fruitful Innovation.

kairos Jesus was announcing was the good news that we can become part of that new Covenant and Kingdom by repenting and believing.

The word *repent* is not merely about feeling bad about things we have done wrong, as is often assumed. This Greek word, *metanoia*, literally means to undergo a change of mind, to gain a new perspective. When Jesus calls people to repent, he is inviting us to open ourselves to a new point of view—God's point of view. The best way to gain that point of view is to listen to what Jesus is saying to us. The first step down the road to repentance is asking yourself and discussing with others the crucial question, "Jesus, what are you saying to me?" This question might seem overly simple and obvious, but it is amazing how different your life becomes when you start genuinely asking that question on a regular basis and when you are open to the input of others to help you answer it accurately.

Jesus did not call people to follow him in isolation, but in community. He called twelve people to repent and believe together with him. This shows us that this question is not meant to be answered alone, but with the direction of our rabbi and the input of our fellow disciples. As we allow the person discipling us to speak into our lives, along with those who are sharing this journey with us, we will begin to discern Jesus' voice speaking to us more clearly, even among all the other voices in our life. When he described himself as the good shepherd, Jesus explained that learning to recognize his voice is critical to this journey of discipleship: *"His sheep follow him because they know his voice"* (John 10:4).

Of course, hearing what Jesus is saying is only half of the process. Once we are able to identify the message Jesus has for us, that message inherently calls for a response. That's why Jesus followed the call to repentance with a call to faith: *repent <u>and believe</u>*. This Greek word, *pisteuo*, is the verb form of the noun we usually translate faith—*pistis*. It means putting faith into action. It describes a relationship in which we trust someone enough to give them control of our lives. We have a problem when it comes to this word in English, because we have no verb form of the noun *faith*. So we use the verb believe in order to convey the active sense of this word, but this is often misunderstood. Believe usually sounds to us like agreeing with an idea or concept, rather than trusting a person.

When Jesus calls us to believe, it is an invitation to trust him enough to act on what he says to us, and to follow where he is leading us. It is best expressed by the crucial second question: "Jesus, what do you want me to do about it?" This is the question of response. It is not something we do out of a sense of obligation, but is a step of faith empowered by the authority of Jesus and the presence of his Spirit within us. As we noted earlier, Paul tells us *"faith comes from hearing, and hearing through the word of Christ"* (Romans 10:17). As we help each other hear clearly what Jesus is saying to each of us, we will also receive the faith we need to respond. This means moving from a hypothetical world and starting to get real. We ask the person discipling us, and our fellow disciples, to help us formulate a concrete plan to put into action what Jesus is calling us to do. Now, the way forward starts to become clearer.

There is a crucial third aspect of this process we might easily miss: accountability. The truth is, even if we hear what Jesus is saying to us and begin to understand what he wants us to do in response, part of us will resist actually doing something about it. This part of us is what Paul refers to as the flesh, rather than the Spirit in us. We need the support and encouragement of our rabbi and fellow disciples to help us overcome the resistance of the flesh and yield to the power of the Spirit. Once a plan starts to take shape, and we have identified the next step Jesus wants us to take, we choose someone to whom we will look for supportive accountability. We follow up with each other using the simple question, "How did it go?" This is not an expression of judgment or pressure, but the loving support and challenge of someone who wants you to become more like Jesus and bear better fruit for his Kingdom.

A very important principle in this process that helps maintain healthy relationships is what we call Low Control/High Accountability. Low control means that we do not have the right to tell anyone what they have to do. That would be manipulative and could lead to all kinds of destructive dynamics. Although we offer each other input and suggestions on what Jesus might be saying and what he might want someone to do, in the end that person alone has to decide how they will respond. Once someone has confirmed what they believe Jesus wants them to do, then it is up to the rabbi and rest of the group to offer the supportive, non-judgmental kind of accountability that will help that person actually take a step of faith and move forward into what God is doing.

We have adapted an incredibly helpful tool to help us remember and pass on the discipling method of Jesus—the LifeShapes Learning Circle:[18]

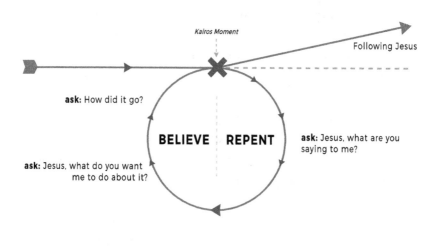

---

18. For an in-depth study of the Circle tool see Mike Breen, *Choosing to Learn from Life* (Pawley's Island: 3DM Publishing, 2015).

A *kairos* moment is an event, large or small, that initiates the process by which Jesus wants to change our perspective on something and move us in a new direction. Repentance means we observe this event and begin to reflect on it by discussing it with others. We ask others to help us answer the question, "Jesus, what are you saying to me?" Believing means we respond by making a plan, establishing accountability, and then stepping out in faith to follow the direction in which Jesus is leading us. Through this process we ask others to help us answer the question, "Jesus what do you want me to do about it?" Those who agree to offer accountability follow up by asking the question, "How did it go?"

This is the process Jesus used to disciple those who would go on to do what he did with others and change the world. He taught them to recognize the times when God's Kingdom was breaking in, gave them a way to discern the significance of these *kairos* moments in their lives, and showed them how to build the kind of small groups where they would get the support and accountability to act on these insights in faith. Any approach to discipleship that claims to follow the way of Jesus must learn how to train people in these basic disciplines of repenting and believing. This is how we are called to become like Jesus and help each other do the same.

13

BECOMING SPIRITUAL PARENTS

CULTURAL TRANSLATION

The word *disciple* (Greek: *mathete*) shows up 232 times in the four Gospels. This gives us an indication of how important the discipling relationship is in the mission of Jesus. Luke uses the term 28 times in the book of Acts while describing the mission of Paul and the other Apostles. However, the word *mathete* does not occur in any of the letters of Paul or the other letters of the New Testament. In Acts Luke repeatedly tells us the leaders of the Jerusalem church multiplied disciples at a tremendous rate and that disciples were active in surrounding cities such as Damascus, Joppa, and Antioch (Acts 6:7; 9:19, 38; 11:26). Furthermore, Luke states very clearly that Paul and Barnabas *made many disciples* on their first missionary journey and that Paul continued to make new disciples and strengthen existing disciples on his subsequent journeys (Acts 14:21; 18:23; 19:9). It is clear from Luke's account that, in the first generation after Jesus' resurrection, disciple continued to be a normative term to describe those who had put their faith in Jesus and were seeking to live according to his teaching and example.

So why is it that Paul and the other New Testament authors didn't use the language of discipleship in their letters? The answer is found in the same kind of cultural disconnect we experience in our modern Western world. As in our world, the Gentile world was largely unfamiliar with the rabbi-disciple relationship. So Paul and the Apostles, to engage with the Gentile world, picked up on another image Jesus used which translated more directly to non-Jewish contexts: the relationship between parents and their children (Mark 10:24; John 13:33; 21:5). In one of his earliest letters, Paul addresses his disciples in Thessalonica this way, *"But we were gentle among you, like a nursing mother taking care of her own children. So, being affectionately desirous of you, we were ready to share with you not only the gospel of God but also our own selves, because you had become very dear to us... For you know how, like a father with his children, we exhorted each one of you and encouraged you and charged you to walk in a manner worthy of God, who calls you into his own kingdom and glory."* (1 Thessalonians 2:7-12)

In the Greek and Roman world, children received their basic instruction in a primary school, traditionally known as a *Ludus Litterarius*, similar to the *Beth Sefer* of the Jewish community. Like their Jewish counterparts, by the age of ten or twelve most of these Greek or Roman children finished their formal education and returned home to learn the extended family business from their parents. A boy stood by his father as he carried out the family trade, watching and observing. Soon his father invited him to begin helping, taking on more responsibility as his skills grew. Eventually, the son became fully engaged in the family trade under the father's supervision. A girl went through the same process with her mother to be trained in the management of the household. The goal of this parental apprenticeship was for the children to learn to do everything their parents did, so they could carry on the family business and pass it on to their own children.

The parallels with discipleship are obvious and striking. It was a brilliant strategy of cross-cultural translation for Paul and the other apostles to adopt the language of spiritual parenthood to communicate the process of discipleship to a Gentile world. Paul uses this imagery to describe his relationship with the believers in Corinth: *"I became your father in Christ Jesus through the gospel. I urge you, then, be imitators of me. That is why I sent you Timothy, my beloved and faithful child in the Lord, to remind you of my ways in Christ, as I teach them everywhere in every church"* (1 Corinthians 4:15-17). Here we see the generations of discipleship expressed in familial terms, as Paul sent his disciple Timothy to continue discipling the Corinthians by imitating his example.

SPIRITUAL PARENTING

Do you have spiritual parents? Are you growing up to become a spiritual parent yourself? These are the questions Paul's example raises those who claim to follow Jesus. Those of us who are raising biological children know our kids need healthy doses of both unconditional love and clear direction. They thrive when they know we will love and accept them no matter what. They also need to know what we expect of them. The same is true for our spiritual children. If discipleship is a kind of spiritual parenting, we need to learn how to create an environment where our spiritual children can *"grow up in every way into him who is the head, into Christ"* (Ephesians 4:15).

We have seen that repenting and believing was central to the way Jesus trained his disciples to hear and respond to his call. In so doing, he created what we call a High Invitation/High Challenge culture. Jesus invited his disciples into the closest kind of relationship, giving them full access to himself and investing everything he had in their lives. At the same time, he challenged them to be willing to give everything and lay down their very lives for the sake of God's Kingdom. This synergistic combination of Covenant invitation and Kingdom challenge empowered the disciples to quickly learn how to do the things Jesus did.

As Jesus concluded his Galilean ministry and prepared to head toward his final destiny in Jerusalem, he took his disciples on a retreat to a city in the far northern region of Israel, Caesarea Philippi. There he asked them,

"'Who do you say I am?' Simon Peter answered, 'You are the Messiah, the Son of the living God.'" (Matthew 16:15-16) Jesus responded to Simon's profession of faith with a huge Covenantal invitation. He gave him a new name, Peter, which means little rock. In the Old Testament, God is repeatedly referred to using this metaphor in passages such as, *"The LORD is my rock, my fortress and my deliverer; my God is my rock, in whom I take refuge, my shield and the horn of my salvation, my stronghold."* (Psalm 18:2)

> Do you have spiritual parents? Are you growing up to become a spiritual parent yourself? These are the questions Paul's example raises those who claim to follow Jesus.

Jesus gave Simon his own name, as clear an invitation to oneness in Covenant as when a bride and groom decide to share the same name. As if that weren't enough, then Jesus went on to entrust Peter with the metaphorical keys to his Kingdom. Jesus was saying to Simon, "Everything I have, I give to you." While Peter and the disciples were still basking in the glow of this incredible invitation, Jesus went on to describe his imminent suffering and death in Jerusalem. When Peter rebuked his Rabbi for this prediction, Jesus said, *"Get behind me Satan!"* He then went on to give all his followers the ultimate challenge: *"Whoever wants to be my disciple must deny themselves and take up their cross and follow me"* (Matthew 16:24). Now he asks them to give him their very lives in return! Jesus' synergistic combination of Covenantal invitation and Kingdom challenge propelled the disciples to become like their Rabbi.

THE HORSE WHISPERER

Monty Roberts grew up in Salinas, California, watching his father train horses with a kind of coercive violence that he saw reflected in his dad's parenting techniques as well. At the age of thirteen, Monty was helping to round up wild horses in Nevada and began to carefully observe the way wild Mustangs interacted. He noticed that when a lone Mustang wanted to join up with a herd, it would first be challenged by the lead mare. She

EMPOWERING MISSIONAL DISCIPLES

would come out of the herd, face the new horse, and give direct eye contact with ears forward and shoulders square, in an aggressive stance. In response the new Mustang would bow its head, avert its gaze, and paw the ground, submissively licking and chewing with its mouth. At this the lead mare then turned sideways, exposing her vulnerable flank, and invited the new horse to draw closer. When the Mustang began to approach, the lead mare again turned to face the new horse in a challenging stance. When the Mustang began bowing and pawing, the lead mare again turned her flank, inviting the new horse in, and so the dance would continue until the new mustang was fully embraced by the herd

This dance of alternating invitation and challenge is what Roberts came to call "speaking Equus."[19] It revolutionized the world of horse training. Instead of coercively forcing a wild horse to submit to the trainer, Roberts developed a technique by which the trainer learns to calibrate the appropriate level of both invitation and challenge to invite the animal into a partnership between horse and rider. Using this approach Roberts is able to break a wild horse, not by tying them to a post for hours and beating them into submission, but by employing this conversation and, in a matter of minutes, introducing both saddle and rider to the horse.

When you read the Gospels and take special note of how Jesus interacted with his disciples, you can see this is very much the way he trained them! Jesus constantly invited the disciples to come close to him, receive all he had to offer, and ultimately to be counted as a part of his own family. At the same time, Jesus regularly challenged the disciples to follow his example of listening to the Father, acting boldly in faith, and laying down his life for the sake of others. The invitation Jesus gave them was to Covenantal relationship, and the challenge he offered was to Kingdom represenation. This calibration of Covenantal invitation and Kingdom challenge is the way Jesus led his disciples through the process of repenting and believing. They

---

19. Monty Roberts, *The Man Who Listens to Horses* (New York: Random House, 1997).

were empowered to keep taking steps of faith by claiming their true identity and exercising their Father's authority. In this way, they imitated Jesus
and ultimately learned to innovate this process with those they discipled.

INVITATION AND CHALLENGE

Jesus' ability to discern how much Covenantal invitation and Kingdom
challenge each of his disciples needed at any given time produced a discipling culture. This culture in turn produced generations of followers who
could do what he did and pass this on to others. At its heart this discipling
culture is empowered by the biblical DNA of Covenant and Kingdom. We
use this matrix to illustrate the four types of cultures created by the way we
calibrate Invitation and Challenge:[20]

If someone fails to invite you into a supportive relationship and also chooses
not to challenge you in any way, it creates a very boring culture. The message is that this person does not care about you enough to even notice. This
is a Low Invitation/Low Challenge environment. We see this in churches

---

20.   Breen, *Building a Discipling Culture*, p. 18.

where survival is the goal and maintenance is the mode. This stagnant environment bores people to tears and does not produce leaders who can generate Kingdom movement.

> The invitation Jesus gave them was to Covenantal relationship, and the challenge he offered was to Kingdom represenation.

If someone offers you all the investment and resources you need, but never really challenges you, it creates a very cozy culture. This puts you in the role of a consumer. It is what we call a High Invitation/Low Challenge environment. Churches that focus on trying to attract new people through their staff-led programs and services tend to produce this culture, regardless of their stated purpose. Members often love this environment because it meets so many of their perceived needs, but it often is not sustainable and inevitably will burn out the leaders.

If someone presents you with a very high level of challenge but does not offer a corresponding invitation to supportive relationship, it produces a very stressful culture. Many people in the corporate world experience this dynamic—they cut your staff and your budget, but increase your quota! We call it a Low Invitation/High Challenge environment. These are the churches where the preachers are calling their members to a life of obedience and sacrifice, but offer little or no help on how to do that in a way that brings good fruit and abundant life. This stress is often expressed through legalism, striving, and judgment.

The life Jesus offered is represented by the remaining quadrant—a High Invitation/High Challenge environment that produces a discipling culture. Jesus made an incredibly high level of investment in people's lives, while at the same time calling them to ideals and purposes far beyond their own ability and strength. This combination is energizing and dynamic— kind of like mixing two volatile chemicals! We want to live a life of greater significance and meaning, but usually don't know how to do it and feel inadequate to the task. Jesus offered people both a life of eternal significance

(Kingdom) and the relational resources that would empower them to live that life (Covenant). This is how Jesus made disciples who could do what he did and who could train others to do the same.

INVITED INTO CHALLENGE

The first time I heard Mike Breen teach, God stirred my heart. Mike described the life of Jesus and the vision of his Kingdom in a way that resonated with my reading of Scripture and my experiences of ministry in a fresh and powerful way. I knew what he was talking about was what I was looking for, so I pursued opportunities to learn more from him. However, unlike other well-known speakers I had interacted with, when I got to spend time with Mike, he didn't put up self-protective barriers. He invited me into his life. He engaged me in genuine theological discussion. He asked about my marriage, my family, and real life. He and his wife Sally welcomed us into their home. We met their adult children. In the midst of it all, Mike told me very directly that I could be as connected to him and what he was doing as I wanted. It was up to me to decide how close I would be. It was a very generous Covenantal invitation.

As I responded to that invitation and started to participate in the movement Mike was building, I was aware of a dynamic I had not experienced in my adult life. In small group conversations with others, Mike asked me difficult questions. He pressed me on issues I might be avoiding. He suggested I do things that were out of my comfort zone. Sometimes these conversations made me uncomfortable. Sometimes they made me mad. But I knew these were conversations I needed to have, and that no one else was willing to have them with me. The Kingdom challenge Mike brought in my life came with such strong Covenantal invitation that I was able to receive the difficult things he was speaking into my life. As I allowed the Spirit of God to work through these conversations and this relationship, I found myself changing. My walk with Jesus grew deeper. My marriage improved. I was closer to my kids. I was becoming a more effective leader.

Eight years later I can honestly say my life has profoundly changed for the better because I have been part of a discipling culture where spiritual parents have offered both invitation and challenge to me in love. In turn, I have been learning how to calibrate invitation and challenge more effectively with the people God has put in my life. As spiritual parents, Pam and I have been developing this culture in our marriage, with our family, in our extended spiritual family, and in the church we have led. The result has been a far healthier, more mature, and more fruitful community of disciples who are learning to live more of the life Jesus modeled for us.

Just as Jesus offered both invitation and challenge to his disciples, they in turn learned how to function as spiritual parents and do the same thing with their spiritual children. We can see this again and again in the letters of Paul. In the midst of division and conflict, he offers clear invitation and strong challenge to the people of Corinth: *"I do not write these things to make you ashamed, but to admonish you as my beloved children... Some are arrogant, as though I were not coming to you. But I will come to you soon, if the Lord wills, and I will find out not the talk of these arrogant people but their power. For the kingdom of God does not consist in talk but in power. What do you wish? Shall I come to you with a rod, or with love in a spirit of gentleness?"* (1 Corinthians 4:14, 18-21).

Jesus and his followers used this careful calibration of Covenantal invitation and Kingdom challenge to create a discipling culture that motivated people to give up everything in order to follow him. It was the kind of environment where his followers didn't just learn to recite theological ideas, to follow religious rituals, or even to observe ethical principles. It was the kind of environment that transformed and empowered simple, ordinary people to become the kind of people who can change the world!

> The Kingdom challenge Mike brought in my life came with such strong Covenantal invitation that I was able to receive the difficult things he was speaking into my life.

14

A VEHICLE FOR DISCIPLESHIP

WHAT KIND OF CAR ARE YOU DRIVING?

I've owned eleven different cars in my lifetime. Six were given to me, four I bought used, and one I bought new. The ones we inherited or were given to us were a huge blessing and often had sentimental value, but didn't necessarily fit our lifestyle. When I was an intern pastor and basically broke, our only car died, and my mom graciously gave us her 1988 Toyota Corolla FX hatchback. It was in good shape, ran like a top, and was an amazing answer to our prayers. The only drawback: it was not exactly designed for our needs.

We had two young boys and were working with students. The Corolla was designed as a fuel-efficient commuter car for 2 and a half passengers, and it had a cargo area big enough for three bags of groceries. Anyone with young kids knows it takes a caravan of camels to carry all the "necessary" equipment to keep children happy and healthy. We could barely squeeze two child seats in the backseat. Try adding in a couple of teenagers who need a ride to youth group—it was impossible. Every summer, loading up the family and gear to drive the 1200 miles to our family cabin in Montana was like packing sardines. In fact, our nickname for the car became the tuna can!

When I got a job with enough income to buy a new car, we decided it was time to take the plunge. So we bought a brand-new 1998 Toyota Sienna minivan. To us there was nothing mini about it—it felt like a Rolls Royce stretch limo. The boys each had their own captain's chair, which meant they couldn't hit each other without a light saber. We could drown out the sounds in the back with Dolby Surround Sound audio. There was room for all our summer vacation necessities, including the rubber raft and snorkel gear. We could fill the minivan up with teenagers when necessary, and I could slide my nine-foot surfboard right between the seats. I thought we had died and gone to heaven! It's a wonderful thing to have a vehicle that meets the needs of your way of life.

For my entire ministry, I have sought an effective vehicle for discipleship. Over the years I spent a lot of time and energy designing processes meant to help people mature as followers of Jesus and bear more and better fruit for his Kingdom. Some people were able to squeeze into the back seat of these vehicles and go on the journey with us, but many people did not. Most were content to attend our worship services and maybe an occasional program at the church, but would or could not participate in an active, intentional process of discipleship. It was a painful, but ultimately liberating experience, to realize the vehicles for discipleship we had developed looked nothing like Jesus' discipling vehicle.

What is your primary method for multiplying disciples who are learning to live the life Jesus modeled for us? If you have an intentional vehicle for discipleship, how is that vehicle working for you? Do you find your disciples are actually learning how to do the things Jesus did? Do you find they are able to pass this on to others? Are these kinds of disciples multiplying in your community? If not, maybe you need a better vehicle. Maybe you have been trying to fit car seats and baby strollers into a compact hatchback, when what you really need is a van or an SUV. Let's take a closer look at the vehicle Jesus used to multiply disciples who could do the same with others.

JESUS' VEHICLE FOR DISCIPLESHIP

Jesus didn't do things haphazardly or by accident. This is especially true of his discipling strategy. Jesus began making disciples the same way he would later train his disciples to begin—by looking for what he described as people of peace. As Jesus prepared his disciples to go out on mission, he told them, *"Whatever house you enter, first say, 'Peace be to this house!' And if a son of peace is there, your peace will rest upon him. But if not, it will return to you. And remain in the same house, eating and drinking what they provide, for the laborer deserves his wages. Do not go from house to house. Whenever you enter a town and they receive you, eat what is set before you. Heal the sick in it and say to them, 'The kingdom of God has come near to you.' But whenever you enter a town and they do not receive you, go into its streets and say, 'Even the dust of your town that clings to our feet we wipe off against you. Nevertheless know this, that the kingdom of God has come near.'"* (Luke 10:5-11)

Offering your peace (Hebrew: *shalom*) in biblical culture was a warm invitation to friendship. The image of your peace resting on someone is a Middle Eastern idiom describing someone who receives and reciprocates that warm invitation to friendship. Jesus' strategy for discipleship begins simply by looking for friends! A Person of Peace likes you, listens to you, and will serve you. When we find a Person of Peace, Jesus says we are to spend time with them, share meals with them, accept hospitality from

> What is your primary method for multiplying disciples who are learning to live the life Jesus modeled for us? If you have an intentional vehicle for discipleship, how is that vehicle working for you?

them, heal the sick there, and explain the Good News of the Kingdom to them.

As we read the Gospels, we see this is exactly how Jesus begins. John tells us at the time of his baptism there were five men from Galilee who were very open and interested in Jesus, so he spent significant time with them (John 1:35-50). When Jesus returned to Galilee, he ended up staying with two of them, Simon and Andrew, healing Simon's mother-in-law, sharing meals with them, and teaching them about the Kingdom of God (Luke 4:38-41). Jesus' first step in making disciples was looking for and investing in People of Peace.

This approach led to some very unlikely people gathering with Jesus as members of an extended spiritual family in the home of Simon and Andrew. Fishermen. Tax collectors. Prostitutes. Who would have guessed? From this larger group, Jesus intentionally identified a core group of disciples to lead his movement. In fact, he spent all night up on a mountain praying about who should be part of that core. The next morning he came down from the mountain, chose twelve, and invited them to follow him (Luke 6:12-16). There were crowds of people referred to as disciples of Jesus, and he shared life and meals with a houseful of them, but Jesus invested himself most of all in this small group of twelve disciples.

In our day we have sometimes construed discipleship as a one-on-one activity, but this is not the vehicle Jesus used. He sometimes carried on evangelistic conversations with people one-on-one, but rarely if ever interacted with his disciples this way. One individual being trained by another individual is a modern interpreation of discipleship. Jesus always made disciples in the context of community. When he invited people to follow him, he was welcoming them into a family. In Capernaum Jesus' disciples filled up the large home of Simon and Andrew. He chose the Twelve from this extended family to be his core group of disciples. Occasionally he took three of them off by themselves for even more intensive investment, but one-on-one discipleship was foreign to Jesus. To use the sociological terms we introduced earlier, Jesus intentionally chose Personal Space (groups of 6-12 people) as the primary context for his most intentional and fruitful discipling work.

When Jesus called his disciples, he not only invited them to share life with him, but also with each other, multiplying his investment. When Peter got out of the boat and followed Jesus onto the water, the other eleven disciples were watching. When Jesus rebuked Peter for setting his mind on human things and not on divine things, they all learned the same lesson. When the risen Jesus appeared to Thomas and invited him to touch his wounds, it was as if they all put their fingers in his hands and side. The disciples sometimes discussed Jesus' words with one another, and this led them to a deeper understanding of his teaching and way of life. A synergy was at work in this personal space of twelve people that was not possible to achieve either one-on-one or with a crowd of disciples.

One of the dynamics that works especially well in a small group of disciples is repenting and believing—hearing what God is saying and acting on that word in faith. When Jesus was giving Simon his new name in Caesarea Philippi, he described the source of Peter's epiphany: *"For flesh and blood has not revealed this to you, but my Father who is in heaven"* (Matthew 16:15-17). Jesus had been teaching the disciples to recognize the Father's voice, and now Peter was allowing that revelation to give him a new perspective. Peter *repented* (Greek: *metanoia*).

Likewise, Jesus followed up on this revelatory insight by challenging all twelve disciples to respond in faith (*believe*) by taking up their cross and following Jesus to Golgotha and beyond (Greek: *pisteuo*). Because Jesus had narrowed his group of disciples to twelve people, he was able to help

> One individual being trained by another individual is a modern interpreation of discipleship. Jesus always made disciples in the context of community. When he invited people to follow him, he was welcoming them into a family.

each of them recognize what God was saying and challenge each to respond by taking a step of faith. Not only that, but there is also built-in accountability for a group of people who live together and share life together. Everyone in Jesus' inner circle knew it would be obvious to the others whether they actually put Jesus' words into practice. A small group of people who speak the truth in love to one another can offer the kind of accountability that empowers us to follow through on responding to what God is saying.

Jesus carried out intentional discipleship in Personal Space because it was the context best suited to offer effective Covenant invitation and Kingdom challenge. After Jesus taught the crowds the parable of the sower and the soils, his closest disciples asked him about it. Jesus proceeded to invite them in closer by explaining in detail the meaning of the sower, the seed, and the four types of soil (Mark 4:1-20). In addition to supportive invitation, Jesus could also offer a level of challenge to the Twelve that is not possible with larger groups. When James and John asked for privileged positions in Jesus' coming Kingdom, he responded, *"You do not know what you are asking. Are you able to drink the cup that I drink, or to be baptized with the baptism with which I am baptized?"* Then he went on to tell them they would all have to lay down their lives just as he was about to do (Mark 10:35-45).

It was no accident Jesus chose a small group of people, invited them into every aspect of his life, and invested everything he had in them. This small group provided an opportunity for Jesus to teach them how to hear from God and respond in faith. It was a setting where he could offer both supportive invitation and empowering challenge. It was a small enough group for genuine trust to develop. The synergy of the group dynamics multiplied Jesus' investment and set the pattern for the disciples to do the same with others, as they followed in the footsteps of their Rabbi. This was Jesus' vehicle for discipleship. If we are going to learn how to make disciples the way he did, we will learn how to form the same kind of vehicle for discipleship in our context.

A DISCIPLING VEHICLE FOR TODAY

As a football player, I always appreciated the importance of the huddle. Eleven guys come together to catch their breath, hear from their leader, and consider what it means for each of them. Then they go out together and put the plan

into action to win the game. Without the huddle we would not have the opportunity to hear clearly what we are supposed to do. Each of us would be trying to figure it out on our own, and we would be pulling in different directions, probably undermining each other's efforts in the process. A huddle is not as critical for the defense, which primarily responds to what is happening on the field, but it is crucial for the offense that seeks to advance the ball and gain ground. A successful football team must have effective huddles.

In our movement, we call our primary vehicle for discipleship Huddles for these reasons. Because the process of discipleship is not familiar in modern Western culture, we need an intentional way to relearn this process as Jesus did it and develop the same types of relationships he had. A Huddle offers the opportunity to spend time with a small group of disciples, helping each other repent and believe. By listening for Jesus' Word and working our way around the Repent and Believe Circle together, we gain a better understanding of how God is speaking to us, and we have a lot more resources to help put that word into practice.

Huddles are typically comprised of 5-8 people who are invited to come together regularly under the leadership of someone with more experience, for the express purpose of becoming the kind of disciples who can in turn disciple others. The goal of a Huddle is to multiply leaders who will build a discipling culture that empowers people to live a more fruitful missional life. Typically, Huddles will meet on a weekly basis for the first year, with seasonal breaks for rest. As the members of a Huddle mature and begin to invite others into a new Huddle which they lead, the original Huddle often moves to every other week, allowing more space for the new Huddles that are multiplying. Eventually, the orbit of the original Huddle widens and becomes an ongoing discipling relationship without the structure of a formally scheduled group.

A Huddle is not discipleship. Meeting together as a Huddle is not discipleship. Active mentoring relationships focused on intentionally helping us become more like Jesus in community are what we call biblical discipleship. A Huddle is simply a vehicle to help us learn how to develop and multiply these kinds of discipling relationships. The time we spend with people outside of our Huddle is critical to the process of discipleship. It doesn't happen in one sixty-minute meeting per week. But we need the organizational structure of a regularly scheduled Huddle to establish discipling relationships and train those we are discipling to do the same with others. As those relationships mature, the formal Huddle will become less important than the mentoring that happens naturally in the context of a wider spiritual family.

Huddles are rooted in the Word of God and often begin by reflecting on Scripture or biblical principles. However, unlike a typical Bible study, the focus is not on acquiring more biblical knowledge—instead, it's on putting God's Word into practice by faith. The leader of a Huddle will begin by presenting whatever content they discern God is leading them to share. Then they will ask each group member to listen for their personal *kairos* by simply **observing** the thing God seems to be bringing to their attention. The Huddle leader typically follows this by inviting each person to briefly **reflect** on their *kairos* and then begins to facilitate a **discussion** aimed at clarifying what God is saying to each person. This leads to the formulation of concrete personal **plans** which are supported by the **accountability** of the leader and the members of the Huddle. This process helps people to **act** in faith on what God has said to them. It is a low-control environment where each person gets to ultimately decide what God is calling him or her to do, but it is also a high-accountability environment where people care enough to follow up and ask how implementation of the plan went.

The Huddle leader seeks to develop a high-invitation, high-challenge environment, where there is a lot of personal investment, along with a clear call to take (what can feel like) risky steps of faith. Because the members of the Huddle know they are loved and are being given effective tools, they experience high challenge as an energizing opportunity to become more fruitful for the Kingdom of God. This level of personal investment means the relationships formed in a Huddle must go beyond the weekly meetings and become true friendships that grow into extended spiritual family. The time spent together outside of the scheduled meetings of the Huddle is just as important, if not more, than the time spent in the weekly meetings. A Huddle is not discipleship; it is a vehicle meant to facilitate the formation of genuine, Jesus-shaped discipling relationships.

Although I was an experienced leader with lots of confidence, when it came to actually leading my first Huddle, I was really intimidated. I had led countless small group meetings, but this was different. I didn't know quite how to incorporate biblical content with the discipling tools I had been given. I wasn't sure how to listen for direct revelation while leading the group. I was concerned that speaking challenging input into someone's life would come across as judgmental and controlling. I wondered if help-

> A Huddle is not discipleship. Meeting together as a Huddle is not discipleship. Active mentoring relationships focused on intentionally helping us become more like Jesus in community are what we call biblical discipleship. A Huddle is simply a vehicle to help us learn how to develop and multiply these kinds of discipling relationships.

ing someone formulate a concrete plan would feel forced and promote legalism. Needless to say, my first few Huddle sessions didn't go so well. My main problem was that I had not yet joined a Huddle myself. I assumed that just hearing or reading about this was enough to learn how to do it. I did not yet understand that discipleship involves more than just information—I needed someone to imitate.

When I finally joined a Huddle myself, I discovered how different it was from the small groups I had led over the previous two decades. Rather than an open discussion on an interesting subject, I realized my Huddle leader was intentionally listening for, and expecting, the Holy Spirit to bring fresh revelation specifically for me and my situation. Rather than simply teaching the content of a biblical passage, my Huddle leader was engaging me in a real process of discernment about what God was saying and how he might want me to respond. Rather than just affirming my theological reflections, my Huddle leader was speaking directly into my life— asking questions, offering input, and challenging me to take a step of faith.

Along with this challenge, my Huddle leader also offered the practical tools and personal support I needed to take the risk of acting on what God was saying. Although my Huddle leader was listening to God and challenging me, it never felt controlling or manipulative. He used language like "I sense God might be saying..." and "I wonder if God wants you to do..." It invited me into a direct encounter with Jesus and gave me the freedom to respond with whatever faith God was giving me. It was energizing, transformational, and empowering!

Once I humbled myself and submitted to the process of discipleship myself by joining a Huddle, everything changed. Now I had a living example to follow. Now I had someone I could ask questions and who offered practical insight. As I received intentional discipleship, I found I was able to give it to others far more effectively. Leading my Huddle became an exciting experience of revelation and brought the joy of seeing God work in the lives of people I love. Now, having lead many hundreds of Huddle sessions,

I continue to feel that same energy and joy that comes from experiencing God's Spirit speaking and moving to make us more like Jesus.

What is your vehicle for discipleship? What kind of fruit is it producing? Is it based on the way Jesus discipled people? Are the people you are discipling able to do the same with others? Is it creating a discipling culture that produces missional movement? If your answer to any of these questions is dissatisfying, then I invite you to come experience our vehicle for discipleship. Not just to read about it, but to experience it for yourself.

All over the world today, thousands of Christian leaders from diverse cultures and backgrounds are engaging in this process through online and local Huddles. In turn, they are discipling tens of thousands of people in their own communities using this lightweight, low-maintenance vehicle to develop a lifestyle of Jesus-shaped discipleship. From the concrete jungle of New York City to the verdant jungles of the Amazon, from the snowy streets of Denmark to the sunny boulevards of Australia, ordinary people just like you and me are becoming and making disciples using this vehicle. Don't think that reading this book is enough, any more than reading a flight manual would prepare you to fly a plane. You need to receive discipleship in order to effectively disciple others. You need to be in a Huddle in order to effectively form and lead a Huddle. 3DMovements exists to offer discipleship to leaders so they can effectively disciple leaders in their context.[21]

> Once I humbled myself and submitted to the process of discipleship myself by joining a Huddle, everything changed. Now I had a living example to follow. Now I had someone I could ask questions and who offered practical insight. As I received intentional discipleship, I found I was able to give it to others far more effectively.

---

21. For information on how to join a 3DM Coaching Huddle, visit 3dmovements.com/coaching.

15

SHEEP / SHEPHERDS

THE POWER OF MULTIPLICATION

When I was in high school, I spent a summer working on a cattle ranch that was home to about four hundred head of Black Angus. There I met an ancient ranch hand who had worked for the owners most of his life. Harold came from Norway, and over the years he had formed a special bond with the herd of cattle raised on the ranch. By the time I knew him Harold was in his 80s, and as far as I could tell, his sole responsibility was moving the herd from one pasture to another. Harold was uniquely qualified for this role because of the cow call he had developed over the years. We were never sure if he was calling "Cow Boss!" or "Come Bess!"

One day I was working a field on a hill that rose above the rest of the ranch, and I saw Harold far down in the valley below, opening a gate through which he intended to lead hundreds of cattle to fresh grazing land. From the vantage point on my tractor, the cattle in question looked like black dots spread out across the huge green field, as if some giant had sprinkled coarse-ground pepper on his salad. I turned the tractor off just in time to hear Harold's one-of-a-kind cow call ringing out across the valley.

Whatever he was saying, as soon as the sound of his voice reached the herd, five hundred munching black heads popped up from the grass, and one thousand fuzzy black ears turned toward him in unison. Again Harold called out, "Co' Boss!" and five hundred cows took a step in his direction. When the first cow reached him, Harold turned around and started walking toward the open gate, all the time calling over his shoulder, "Co' Boss!" As the one cow began to follow Harold, three others moved into position behind that one. Then three for four more pulled up behind each of those three. Soon those ten had five more behind them. Before long the entire heard was following Harold, one behind another, spreading out in a huge delta-shaped mass across the field. From my tractor seat up on the hill, it looked like old Harold was dragging the world's largest black blanket across that field and through the little gate.

In much the same way, Jesus' life of discipleship taps into the power of multiplication. Because each cow set an example that several other cows followed, old Harold was able to lead 250 tons of beef by simply calling to them and showing them the way. Jesus described himself as the good shepherd and then said, *"The sheep hear his voice, and he calls his own sheep by name and leads them out. When he has brought out all his own, he goes before them, and the sheep follow him, for they know his voice."* (John 10:3-4) Those who follow the Good Shepherd are called to help others recognize his voice and follow him as well.

In our movement we like to say that followers of Jesus are meant to look like a sheep from the front and a shepherd from the back. Disciples look like a sheep from the front because they are following someone who is helping them learn how to follow Jesus. Likewise, they look like a shepherd from the back because they are helping others learn how to follow Jesus.

The way Paul said it was, *"Be imitators of me, as I am of Christ."* (1 Corinthians 11:1) Being a disciple of Jesus means being committed to learning from someone else how to effectively invest your life in others so they will learn to do the same. Sheep-shepherds multiply the movement of Jesus.

We all need a real-life example to follow—a flesh-and-blood person who can help us learn to live the life Jesus modeled for us. However, it is important to remember that our present-day examples will always be imperfect. The call to make disciples is a call to point people toward Jesus by the fallible example of our lives. If people are only imitating us, they will get a degraded version of Jesus. Have you ever gone to a copy machine and tried to make a copy of a copy of a copy of a copy of a copy? The picture gets muddled and the text starts to blur into obscurity. As we welcome people into our lives and invite them to follow us as we follow Jesus, it is always the Jesus in us we are pointing them toward, not ourselves. No matter who is discipling us, the goal is always to become a more mature disciple of Jesus.

It can be intimidating when we hear the challenge to disciple others in this way. Most of us feel unworthy of setting an example for others. But the truth is, people don't need a perfect example of Jesus—they just need a living example. Paul wouldn't let Timothy use his age as an excuse for not inviting people to imitate him: *"Let no one despise you for your youth, but set the believers an example in speech, in conduct, in love, in faith, in purity."* (1 Timothy 4:12) By being open about our shortcomings and submitting to the journey of discipleship ourselves, we will be able to offer those who follow us a real-life example of Jesus they can actually imitate. Discipleship is not for the elite or the super-spiritual—it is for ordinary people just like you and me! I like the way the famous first-century Rabbi Hillel said it: "God can make a disciple out of anyone."

A MULTIPLYING MOVEMENT

Jesus consistently drew huge crowds who came to hear him teach and watch him perform miracles, but in the end Luke tells us there were only 120 disciples who persevered and gathered in the Upper Room in Jerusalem on Pentecost. To the casual observer, it might appear as if Jesus' teaching and ministry didn't amount to much. After all, how could 120 people make a significant impact on the world? A more careful observer would recognize these 120 men and women were sheep-shepherds who carried within them the DNA of a multiplying movement that would indeed change the world!

In Luke 9 we read about Jesus sending his twelve disciples out on mission to do the things they had been watching and helping him do. In Luke 10 we read of Jesus gathering 72 of his disciples, training and sending them out on mission as well. The only clue we have about who these people are is the repeated description of Jesus gathering at the house of Simon and Andrew in Capernaum with a houseful of disciples that he called his extended family. Is this the 72 who are sent out? It is interesting to realize that if each of the twelve disciples were to invest in six other members of Jesus' extended family, it would add up to 72 people plus the Twelve. The Gospels are not explicit about this, so we can't know for sure if this was the second generation of disciples, but we can be sure the original disciples learned how to disciple others who learned to do the same and so fulfilled the Great Commission.

> Disciples look like a sheep from the front because they are following someone who is helping them learn how to follow Jesus. Likewise, they look like a shepherd from the back because they are helping others learn how to follow Jesus.

When we read on in the Acts of the Apostles and the letters of Paul, it becomes clear the newly converted Saul of Tarsus was not discipled by any of the original twelve disciples. Ananias and Barnabas and other followers of Jesus in Damascus were the ones God used to help Saul begin his walk with Jesus. Perhaps they were discipled by one of the twelve disciples or, more likely, by one of the 72 disciples. That means Saul already represents a third or fourth generation of Jesus' disciples. Now think about some of the people Paul discipled who in turn invested themselves in the lives of other disciples: Silas, Timothy, Luke, Titus, Lydia, Aquila, Priscilla, Epaphras, Phoebe, Epaphroditus, Euodia, Syntyche, Clement, Philemon, Apphia, Archippus, Onesimus, Aristarchus, Sosthenes, Stephanas, Fortunatus, Onesiphorus, and Achaicus.

Paul was very clear that his spiritual children were called to reproduce the life of Jesus in other disciples who would, in turn, do the same with yet others. Writing to his disciple Timothy, he said, *"You then, my child, be strengthened by the grace that is in Christ Jesus, and what you have heard from me in the presence of many witnesses entrust to faithful people who will be able to teach others also."* (2 Timothy 2:1-2) If each of those in this abbreviated list of Paul's followers discipled six others who, in turn, did the same, the direct fruit of discipleship in Paul's lifetime would be well over 5,000 disciples—and that is just one branch of Jesus' new family tree.

By training and empowering his disciples to do with others what he did with them, Jesus built the principle of multiplication into the very DNA of his movement. Amazingly, within a few months of Jesus' death and resurrection, the number of Jesus' disciples had swelled into the thousands (Acts 1:15; 2:41; 4:4). By the time the church in Jerusalem was scattered and Paul began his missionary journeys, the seeds of Jesus' movement were being planted all across the Mediterranean world. Because each one carried the DNA of Jesus' discipling culture, these seeds multiplied time and time again. By the time Emperor Constantine legalized Christianity in AD 313, the movement Jesus began had reached over half the Roman Empire. No matter how much pressure or persecution was brought to bear against the leaders of this movement, more and more lives continued to be transformed by the power of God working through those willing to invest in the lives of others and welcome them into a missional family. Today God is renewing this transformational movement through the rediscovery of discipleship and mission as a way of life.

IN SEARCH OF A MENTOR

I have been a Christian for over 30 years now, but throughout those three decades no one intentionally discipled me until I joined 3DMovements. When I came to Christ during my high school years, my pastor and youth director had a significant impact on my life. They taught me about Jesus and the Bible, and I was influenced by their example, for which I am deeply grateful. They gave me opportunities to lead, but they were not trained to disciple leaders, so they did not intentionally build a discipling relationship with me. Over the years many other people in my life have inspired, encouraged, taught, and supported me, but no one ever invited me to follow them. No one ever asked me if I would like to build the kind of relationship with them that Jesus built with his disciples. No one offered to help me learn how to become more like Jesus and do the things he did through their example.

For that reason I never intentionally discipled others. When I heard people talk about discipleship, I always experienced a kind of disconnect. I understood Jesus had disciples and had a vague sense that being a disciple of Jesus meant becoming more like him, but I had no clear sense of how that might happen. As a pastor I taught and preached on discipleship, but I assumed this was something you did on your own, because that's how I had to do it. I became a follower of Jesus by attending worship services and Bible studies, praying, and reading the Bible on my own. Eventually I joined small groups with others who were also trying to learn how to follow Jesus on their own. Even though we read the Bible, discussed its meaning for our lives, and prayed together, no one was intentionally discipling anyone else.

Whenever I heard someone use the word disciple as a verb, it always made me feel a little weird: "So and so is discipling me" or "I am discipling so and so." It sounded presumptuous and kind of cultish. Who are we to disciple anyone? Jesus is the one who makes disciples, not us, right? I never really thought through the logic that if I were to become like Jesus and do the things he did, then I would necessarily have disciples like he did. The first time I heard Mike Breen ask, "Who are your disciples?" I realized that, although I had taught and preached Jesus' Great Commission many times and devoted myself to a life of full-time ministry, I was not intentionally making disciples as he commanded. Sure I was helping people in their walk with Jesus, and by default my life served as an example of this, but it was happening by accident rather than by design. It was implicit at best, but certainly not explicit. I had to come to the sobering realization that I was not following Jesus' example by making disciples the way he made disciples.

Mike went on to describe discipleship as the process of inviting others into your own imperfect life as a living example of Jesus for them to imitate. Then he asked the second mind-blowing question: "Do you have a life others want? Is it a life worth imitating?" I had to admit that in many ways, my busy, stressful, overworked life was probably not appealing to others. Perhaps they might admire my life, but not many people were drawn to emulate the way I was living. I began to realize this is where biblical discipleship begins. I needed someone to disciple me before I could become effective at discipling others. I needed to learn how to live as a sheep-shepherd.

THE COST OF DISCIPLESHIP

Once I realized how much I needed someone to disciple me the way Jesus did, I began to pursue it as a major priority. It wasn't easy because the only people I knew who were willing and able to mentor me into this lifestyle of discipleship lived on the other side of the country. I had to decide how much I was willing to invest in the process. Jesus was shockingly clear about the cost of his way of discipleship: *"If anyone would come after me, let him deny himself and take up his cross and follow me. For whoever would save his life will lose it, but whoever loses his life for my sake will find it."* (Matthew 16:24-25) In the end it cost me my time, energy, relational capacity, intellect, and money. Even more, I had to be willing to put to death my pride and addiction to the comfortable.

If you are going to learn how to disciple leaders who can disciple others into the way of Jesus, it will cost you a lot. Are you willing to open your life to someone else, admit you need help, and submit to that person's leadership as they follow Jesus? Are you willing to address the issues in your own life, marriage, and family, before you begin making changes to your church or organization? Are you willing to learn a new language and master some new tools that will equip you to train others to do the same things you are learning? Are you willing to face some criticism and make some difficult leadership choices in order to see a culture of discipleship begin to take root and grow in your community? Like Jesus said, we need to count the cost.

It is worth carefully counting the cost of discipleship because there is a lot at stake. Dallas Willard explained it this way; "The greatest issue facing the world today, with all its heartbreaking needs, is whether those who, by profession or culture, are identified as 'Christians' will become disciples—students, apprentices, practitioners—of Jesus Christ, steadily learning from him how to live the life of the Kingdom of the Heavens into every corner of human existence."[22] I don't know about you, but I want my life to matter. I want to spend my life on the things that will last for eternity. Discipleship is the decision to invest your life in people, the only part of this creation that will last forever. For that reason discipleship in the way of Jesus is an incredibly good investment.

Dietrich Bonhoeffer was a German pastor living in Berlin during the reign of Hitler who, in spite of the Nazi government's ban against his teaching, chose to invest in young Christian leaders at the underground Finkenwalde Seminary. Although a biblical peace activist and pacifist, he eventually decided to participate in the plot against Hitler's life and ended up paying for it with his own. He was executed by a Nazi firing squad two weeks before the Allies liberated his concentration camp.

---

22. Dallas Willard, *The Great Omission: Reclaiming Jesus's Essential Teachings on Discipleship* (New York: Harper Collins, 2006), Introduction, p. xv.

Bonhoeffer well understood the high cost of following where Jesus leads us, but was emboldened to do so by the priceless grace he had received so freely. Bonhoeffer explained, "Cheap grace is grace without discipleship, grace without the cross, grace without Jesus Christ, living and incarnate. Costly grace is the treasure hidden in the field; for the sake of it a man will go and sell all that he has... Such grace is costly because it calls us to follow, and it is grace because it calls us to follow Jesus Christ. It is costly because it costs a man his life, and it is grace because it gives a man the only true life. It is costly because it condemns sin, and grace because it justifies the sinner. Above all, it is costly because it cost God the life of his Son: 'you were bought at a price,' and what has cost God much cannot be cheap for us. Above all, it is grace because God did not reckon his Son too dear a price to pay for our life, but delivered him up for us."[23]

It is true that discipleship is costly, but it is also true that God's grace overflows our lives with more than enough riches to pay that price. Discipleship is not a heavy burden that we must bear by our own strength—it is the light yoke of a death that leads to true life. Jesus' call to take up our cross comes with the promise of an abundant, overflowing Kingdom life. I have found this to be true without exception and without fail. Whatever cost I had to pay in pursuing the kind of discipleship that would multiply the life of Jesus in others has come back to me one hundred-fold in countless blessings. Whatever investment I have made in the lives of others has produced a return completely out of proportion to what I put in.

With a married son and the potential of becoming a grandparent in the foreseeable future, I have started thinking about the cost of parenthood. If I added up just the financial costs associated with raising our two sons, it would approach half a million dollars... and that doesn't count the emotional, physical, and intellectual costs. But when I look at the value of our relationship with them and with our daughters-in-law, and all they bring

23. Dietrich Bonhoeffer, *The Cost of Discipleship* (New York: Touchstone, 1937, 1959), p. 45.

> Discipleship is not a heavy burden that we must bear by our own strength—it is the light yoke of a death that leads to true life. Jesus' call to take up our cross comes with the promise of an abundant, overflowing Kingdom life.

into our lives, that cost is a just drop in the bucket. When you add on the prospect of grandchildren and great-grandchildren, well there is no comparison! The same is true of our spiritual children, grandchildren, and great-grandchildren.

As I mentioned earlier, I felt very inadequate when I began my first Huddle, but as I trusted Jesus' power to be made perfect in my weakness, I was amazed at what God began to do. Real life-change soon became evident. People came away from our times together with greater boldness to live the life of Jesus in their homes, marriages, and workplaces. They followed through in faith on the things God was calling them to. They grew in awareness of God's power to transform their lives, and better fruit began to multiply in their lives and the lives of those closest to them. They began to invest their lives in others and do with them what they were learning in our Huddle. Now I came away from every Huddle feeling energized and fulfilled because of how significant the investment of time and energy was proving to be. I knew the time and energy I was investing, not just in the Huddle, but in these discipling relationships, was well worth whatever it cost me.

In fact, one woman in that first Huddle soon formed a Huddle of her own and began to disciple a group of women. About six months later, one of the women in that Huddle also formed a Huddle and began investing in another small group of people. One of the women in that Huddle discerned, through the process of repenting and believing, that God was calling her to reach out to Japanese women in our community. Her Huddle leader helped her find a Japanese-language version of Alpha, a course in basic Christianity, and over the following year six Japanese women became followers of Jesus through her investment in them!

Discipleship is the process of raising up spiritual sons and daughters so they are empowered to live a fruitful life by following Jesus and reproducing their own spiritual sons and daughters. Our older son and his wife are expecting their first child and soon we will become biological grandparents for the first time! I know it will be one of the greatest joys of my life to hold my children's children in my arms. I am grateful to say that I am already a spiritual grandfather and great-grandfather many times over, and it is one of the greatest blessings of my life. There is nothing more fulfilling than making disciples who can make disciples and living as part of Jesus family on mission, seeking and saving the lost. Whatever it costs you to produce generations of spiritual great-grandchildren who are following Jesus, it can't be compared to the joy and blessing this kind of fruit brings.

PART 3

MULTIPLYING FAMILIES ON MISSION

16

REDISCOVERING FAMILY

THE BEST TIME OF YEAR

I was born in the same northwestern Montana town as my father and grandfather. Both of my parents grew up in that town. My grandparents on both sides still lived in that town when I was a kid, along with numerous great aunts and uncles, cousins and second cousins—you get the idea. To say I have roots there is an understatement.

However, I did not actually grow up in Montana. My dad was a naval pilot who took a job flying for Pan American Airlines, so we lived in places like Hong Kong and West Berlin when I was a kid. But no matter where we lived in the world, every summer we made our way back to the family cabin on the eastern shore of Flathead Lake, near that same northwestern Montana town. In fact, that is where I am writing this right now.

As I described earlier, my grandfather bought this lakefront property at the end of World War II sight unseen. When he returned home he built a little two-bedroom cabin on that property and  my dad spent his childhood summers there. I spent every summer of my childhood at that little cabin. Our sons have done the same all their lives, and we hope it will be so for generations to come. It has always been the gathering place for our extended family. Since before I can remember, this was the place where my small family of four suddenly swelled to dozens of grandparents, aunts, uncles, cousins, and lifelong friends.

Summer at the lake with extended family was always my favorite time of year. We gathered for meals around a dining table augmented by card tables and folding chairs. We enjoyed taking time to picnic, fish, hike, water ski, play cards, and roast marshmallows over beach fires. The time was filled with conversation, laughter, reports of recent events, and memories of times gone by. Before we knew it, of course, vacation ended, and we scattered to various places where we resumed our "normal" lives.

Something was different and wonderful about being part of a big, extended family, even for just a week or two. There was always someone to talk to or play with. You got to interact with a wide variety of personality types. Multiple generations shared both the wisdom of age and the passion of youth with each other. Lots of hands helped fix meals and clean up afterward. When problems arose plenty of people were there to help solve them. The joy and love seemed to multiply when we were all together. Of course, there were conflicts as well, but somehow the larger extended family was able to overcome whatever challenges it faced.

A BIBLICAL VISION OF FAMILY

What do you think of when you hear the word family? Most of us in the modern western world picture a mom, a dad, and some kids living in a single-family dwelling like a house or apartment. A nuclear family. A modern family. But it has not always been this way.

In the Bible, and in many cultures around the world still today, family means grandparents, aunts, uncles, parents, brothers, sisters, cousins, close friends, and business partners, sharing life and work together. In the Bible this understanding of family is described by the Hebrew word *beth* and the Greek word *oikos*. These words are hard to translate because we don't have the same word in English. They are often translated *house* or *household*, but those words make most modern people think of a nuclear family living in a single-family dwelling.

For biblical people the primary expression of family was not the nuclear family, but the extended family—the *beth / oikos*. To be honest, no one in the ancient world would have been foolish enough to deliberately face the challenges of life with just a nuclear family. If their family had included only one couple and their kids, who would staff the family business? If the parents got sick, who would bring in the crops? If bandits attacked, who would fight them off? When the parents got old, who would care for them? Instinctively they knew they needed a larger family to face and overcome the inevitable challenges that would arise. Furthermore, they knew the larger and stronger their *oikos* was, the more likely they were to be fruitful and prosperous.

The biblical *oikos* was normally built around a common family business. Multiple generations working together in a common vocation could be very successful. For instance, the family business of Simon and Andrew in Capernaum was fishing. This doesn't mean Simon and Andrew each lived in separate houses and kissed their wives goodbye each morning as they went off to work somewhere carrying their lunchboxes. On the contrary, they shared the same extended family home where multiple generations lived and worked together in a common vocation. Some of them knotted nets. Some of them fashioned weights and floats. Some of them cleaned the fish and dried them on the rooftops. Some of them sold the fish in the market. And some of them went out in the boats to catch the fish.

We can see this way of life reflected in the ancient houses of biblical families. One of the indicators of an Israelite settlement is what archaeologists call the four-room house. These homes were comprised of three simple rooms built around a walled, open-air courtyard (the fourth room), and they are always present in the excavations of ancient Israelite settlements. Each of the rooms housed a nuclear family, and together they made up an extended family. This is the *beth* of the Old Testament period and reflects the Israelite practice of multiple generations living and working together.

We see a similar design in Jewish homes from the New Testament period. For instance, archaeologists have identified, with almost complete certainty, the home of Simon and Andrew in Capernaum. It is 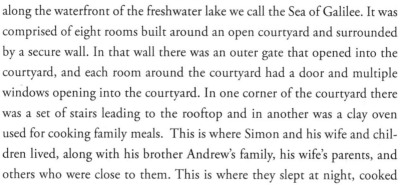 situated one block south of the synagogue along the waterfront of the freshwater lake we call the Sea of Galilee. It was comprised of eight rooms built around an open courtyard and surrounded by a secure wall. In that wall there was an outer gate that opened into the courtyard, and each room around the courtyard had a door and multiple windows opening into the courtyard. In one corner of the courtyard there was a set of stairs leading to the rooftop and in another was a clay oven used for cooking family meals. This is where Simon and his wife and children lived, along with his brother Andrew's family, his wife's parents, and others who were close to them. This is where they slept at night, cooked and ate meals together, and carried out a prosperous fishing business that afforded them a large home in the prime neighborhood of their city.

The biblical *beth* or *oikos* existed for two primary reasons: provision and protection. Living together with multiple nuclear families who could specialize in various aspects of the family business while passing on their knowledge and skills by training up successive generations enabled them to be much more productive and successful in providing for their families. Likewise, when faced with various

> In the Bible, and in many cultures around the world still today, family means grandparents, aunts, uncles, parents, brothers, sisters, cousins, close friends, and business partners, sharing life and work together. In the Bible this understanding of family is described by the Hebrew word *beth* and the Greek word *oikos*.

challenges, the *oikos* was far better equipped to protect the interests of the family. At harvest time a big family was able to bring in the crops before they went to seed in the field. Robbers were much less likely to attack a family if they knew there were six strong men defending the home. In times of political unrest, the *oikos* would bar the outer gate of their walled compound, turning the house into a small fortress. Living only as a nuclear family was a precarious proposition. Living in a strong *oikos* provided for and protected the family.

In our modern world we have developed various systems and structures that have led us to assume we don't need an *oikos*. The industrial revolution led to the rise of corporations that replaced the family business and took parents out of their homes to fulfill their vocation. As people moved from villages and farms into rapidly growing cities, police forces and fire departments were developed to maintain order and protect citizens from disaster. We now pay for things like health insurance, auto insurance, homeowner's insurance, life insurance, workers compensation, and disability to protect ourselves from the inevitable challenges life continues to dish out.

All of this has led us to assume we can thrive with just a nuclear family or even as individuals. Casting off the provision and protection of the *oikos*, we look to modern social structures to provide what we need. One glance at the modern nuclear family might cause us to reassess this assumption. With over 50 percent of marriages ending in divorce, and record numbers of single parents struggling to raise healthy kids in even less than a nuclear family, it is obvious our modern redefinition of the family has put an unbearable strain on what has always been the cornerstone of human community.

This is not to say our modern support structures are to blame, but rather to say they are not enough to replace the strength and health an extended family provides. What a blessing to have the protection of faithful police officers and firefighters! What a blessing to receive insurance funds to rebuild a home after it burns to the ground! But no insurance policy or civic organization can replace the relational resources provided by multiple generations of people who live and work together for their common good. Perhaps it is time for us to reconsider our assumptions about the family, not just for a week or two on summer vacation or every few years at a family reunion. Perhaps we need to rediscover a new kind of family that has been lost to the modern world.

A NEW KIND OF FAMILY

One of the challenges when reading the Bible is the inevitable effect unconscious cultural filters exert on our understanding of its meaning. For instance, as a western American, I have grown up with an intensely individualistic mindset. The cultural vision of the American frontier was rugged individuals persevering against an inhospitable environment and overcoming on their own. My great-grandfather came to Montana as a young man when it was still the Wild West, and he knew he had to make it on his own if he was to survive. You had no one to rely on except yourself. These values have been unconsciously passed down through the generations to me and probably now to my sons.

As a result, for most of my life, when reading the Gospels I automatically thought of Jesus primarily as an individual facing his challenges alone. I didn't think much about Jesus as part of a family. If his family crossed my mind at all, it was only as a nuclear family made up of Joseph, Mary, and Jesus. When I read of Jesus' baptism in the Jordan River, I missed the fact that John the Baptist was part of Jesus' extended family. When I read of Jesus preaching in his hometown synagogue, I never thought of his relatives being there. When I read of Jesus calling disciples, I only thought of them as individuals, and the people they ministered to as individuals. But this cultural filter of individualism blinded me to the profound importance of family in the life and ministry of Jesus. We can't eliminate our cultural filters, but we can become aware of them, adjust our perspective accordingly, and discover what we have been missing.

Luke 4 describes Jesus beginning his ministry by returning to his hometown of Nazareth following his baptism and time of testing in the wilderness. Until I spent time in Nazareth, I never thought to consider where Jesus stayed upon his return. Luke doesn't specify, because in that culture the assumption is that Jesus would return to his *oikos* and stay in one of the rooms of his extended family compound. The Gospels tell us Jesus' family business was that of the *tekton*. This Greek word is often translated *carpenter*, and those of us with northern European cultural filters naturally envision Joseph and Jesus working with the lathe and plane in a woodshop. However, in a Middle Eastern context *tekton* is better translated *builder*, so we should think of the family as contractors who worked primarily in stone, the main building material available. Jesus and his brothers were strong men used to cutting, carrying, and setting blocks of limestone. Herod Antipas' rebuilding of the nearby city of Sepphoris into his new capital during Jesus' boyhood years would have ensured plenty of lucrative business opportunities for the extended family.

When Luke describes Jesus going to his hometown synagogue on the Sabbath day, our individualistic filters might cause us to picture him going there alone. However, in that culture it would be unthinkable for Jesus to go without his *oikos*. He would have gone with his aunts and uncles and mother and brothers and sisters and cousins and anyone else who was living and working as part of that extended family. So when Jesus stood up to read from the scroll of the Prophet Isaiah, we can assume his *oikos* was there in the synagogue with him, excited for this moment when their family member was being recognized as a rabbi by their whole village. Jesus read the powerful messianic promises from Isaiah 61, sat down in the teachers' seat, and dramatically declared, *"Today this Scripture has been fulfilled in your hearing."* (Luke 4:21)

It is hard to overestimate how popular this message would have been with the residents of Nazareth. The Jewish people had been attacked, invaded, occupied, and oppressed for more generations than anyone could remember. The pagan soldiers of a conquering army patrolled their streets, while traitors extorted the crushing taxes that kept Rome at bay and fed the megalomania of Herod's sons. In their context the promise that God was going to set free the oppressed and captives now was incredibly good news! When they heard it, the people in the synagogue marveled at his gracious words and began whispering their admiration and affirmation to each other.

How tempting it must have been for Jesus to stop there and enjoy the adulation. But he went on to tell them the whole truth. Using biblical examples of how God had included and blessed pagan Gentiles in the past, Jesus declared this good news was not just for Jews, but for everyone. Centuries of anger, resentment, and bitterness erupted in rage, and the people dragged Jesus off to one of the cliffs that drop into the Jezreel Valley to the south of Nazareth. The ancient rabbis proscribed that the method of execution for heresy was to bind a person's hands and feet, drop him from a height at least twice that of a man, and if the fall did not kill him, to drop stones on him until he were dead.[24] More than mob violence, this was a

24. Jacob Neusner, editor, *The Mishna: A New Translation* (New Haven: Yale University Press, 1988), Fourth Division: Order of Damages, Sanhedrin, p. 583ff.

deliberate act of execution for heresy, the most extreme form of rejection possible.

Again, my individualistic filters kept me from asking the obvious question: where was Jesus' *oikos* while this is happening? Knowing that *oikos* is about provision and protection, shouldn't Jesus' stonemason uncles, brothers, and cousins stand up for him, ready to fight? Why wasn't his mother clinging to his legs screaming for them not to hurt her son? At the very least, his family members were complicit in rejecting Jesus and his vision for the Good News of the Kingdom. Jesus had come to his own *oikos*, asking them to support his mission, and they utterly rejected him. John describes it this way, *"He came to his own, and his own people did not receive him."* (John 1:11) It is hard to imagine the pain and disappointment he must have felt.

After describing Jesus' mysterious escape from the crowd, Luke tells us Jesus went down to Capernaum, the prosperous fishing town on the north shore of the Sea of Galilee. Why did he go there? In John's account of Jesus' baptism, we hear about five guys from Galilee who showed great interest in Jesus and exhibited a desire to follow him: the brothers Simon and Andrew, along with Philip and Nathaniel. The fifth guy is anonymous, but is probably John, who goes unnamed in his own Gospel. Simon, Andrew, and John were fishermen from Capernaum. It seems Jesus was going to Capernaum to find these guys and begin investing in them as prospective disciples. After teaching in the Capernaum synagogue and delivering a possessed man, Jesus went with Simon and Andrew to their nearby extended family house (*oikos*).

Jesus then did exactly what he later trained his disciples to do when they found people who are open and responsive to them (i.e. People of Peace cf. Luke 10:1-9). First he went with them into their home. Then he healed Simon's mother-in-law. Then he shared in the meal she cooked for them. Jesus was testing the water to see if these guys might be People of Peace who would ultimately follow him. But then Jesus did something completely revolutionary, *"Now when the sun was setting, all those who had any who were sick with various diseases brought them to him, and he laid his hands on every one of them and healed them. And demons also came out of many, crying, 'You are the Son of God!' But he rebuked them and would not allow them to speak, because they knew that he was the Christ."* (Luke 4:40-41)

Remember, *oikos* was designed to provide for and protect the extended family. The *oikos* existed for the sake of the *oikos*. But Jesus did something completely unexpected. Jesus turned the family inside out. The door to the courtyard, which was meant to keep out anyone who was not part of the extended family, was now flung wide open to invite everyone in—even the demon possessed! The message Jesus proclaimed in Nazareth was now coming to fruition in Capernaum. The oppressed were being set free. The blind were receiving their sight. The Kingdom of God was coming! And it was all happening within a new kind of family.

From this point on, the extended family of Simon and Andrew was now described as Jesus' own family. The Gospel writers explicitly refer to the house of Simon and Andrew in Capernaum as Jesus' *oikos* eleven times. Again and again we read of Jesus teaching, healing, and delivering people in this extended family home, which was now his home and family. To reinforce this, all three Synoptic Gospels describe what happened when Jesus' biological family heard rumors he had gone out of his mind. They came to the house of Simon and Andrew in Capernaum to bring him back to the *oikos* in Nazareth. In Mark's words, *"And his mother and his brothers came, and standing outside they sent to him and called him. And a crowd was sitting around him, and they said to him, 'Your mother and your brothers are outside, seeking you.' And he answered them, 'Who are my mother and my brothers?' And looking about at those who sat around him, he said, 'Here are my mother and my brothers! For whoever does the will of God, he is my brother and sister and mother.'"* (Mark 3:31-35)

When we account for our cultural filters and read the Gospels in light of first-century Jewish culture, we begin to see Jesus' mission in a new light. He was not a lone individual facing the challenges of extending God's Kingdom by himself. Jesus did not call his disciples to abandon their families in order to follow him. He and the Twelve did not isolate themselves as they carried out their mission. Quite the contrary, Jesus built a whole new kind of family and invited his followers to carry out God's Kingdom mission as part of that

> Remember, *oikos* was designed to provide for and protect the extended family. The *oikos* existed for the sake of the *oikos*. But Jesus did something completely unexpected. Jesus turned the family inside out.

kind of *oikos*. This new kind of family was not defined primarily by blood or birth, but by a Covenant relationship with God and a Kingdom mission for the world. This new kind of family did not exist primarily to defend and provide for its own members, but to seek and save the lost.

Not a nuclear family, but an extended family. Not only a biological family, but also a spiritual family. Not a family that exists primarily for itself, but a family that exists for others. A Kingdom family. A family on mission!

17

BUILDING A FAMILY ON MISSION

BETTER TOGETHER

I was 21 years old when I first visited Jerusalem. The first person I met there was a young Palestinian Christian named Yousef. Yousef was my age, had been born in the Old City of Jerusalem, and lived there as part of an extended family. Two years later my wife and I spent two months in Israel and Egypt with a group of fellow graduate students, and our friendship with Yousef grew. Another two years later, an academic fellowship allowed me to pursue a year of post-graduate studies in New Testament Archaeology and Sociology at the French School of Biblical Archaeology in Jerusalem. Pam and I and our infant son lived inside the walls of the Old City, just a few minutes' walk from the home of Yousef's extended family, who can trace their ancestry back at least seven hundred years in that very spot!

During that year Yousef began to invite us to gatherings of his extended family. Right away I noticed something fascinating. The design of his family's home was practically identical to the ancient homes I was learning about in my study of New Testament archaeology. The front door was made of thick steel and wrapped with bands of steel reinforcing the hinges. It opened into a large central room that had a high glass ceiling and was furnished with couches, chairs, and a dining table. It was obvious this room used to be an open courtyard, which was later enclosed with a transparent roof. From the central courtyard/room were six doors that gave access to various bedrooms used by different members of the extended family. A narrow corridor gave access to the adjacent kitchen where family meals were prepared. Yousef lived here with his grandparents, parents, brothers and sisters, an aunt and uncle, and cousins, as families had been doing for countless centuries in that place.

As we spent time with Yousef's family, we noticed how the dynamics of multiple nuclear families sharing life together was quite different from our own families of origin. Lots of people were involved in preparing and serving the meals. The kids had grandparents, aunts and uncles, and older cousins to look out for them, in addition to their own parents. The elderly members of the family had lots of people to help them out as well. The conversation and laughter around the table was infectious and joyful. It looked very much like the typical first-century *oikos* I was learning about in my studies. It reminded me of my summer vacations back at the family cabin in Montana—but this was their normal way of life! Pam and I were welcomed as members of the family and have been treated as such ever since, participating in celebrations of baptisms, confirmations, graduations, and the like.

Since then Pam and I have continued to bring Christian pilgrims to the Holy Land on a unique immersion experience we have designed in The Footsteps of Jesus. For over thirty years now, our friendship with Yousef and his extended family has deepened. Yousef married a lovely Christian Palestinian woman from an extended family that has lived for countless generations in the Old City of Jerusalem as well. Yousef's brother married a daughter of that same extended family. Now these two families are interconnected in myriad ways. Recently some of the family members opened a new restaurant in Jerusalem, and it is very good. The first time we went there for dinner, we noticed right away that it was an extended family enterprise. Yousef's brothers-in-law were running the restaurant and tending bar. Yousef's sons and nephews were bussing tables and washing dishes. Although Yousef has a full-time job of his own, he often drops in to the restaurant after work to see if they need any help. When you live in an extended family, it is natural to share vocation together just as you share life together.

A FAMILY BUSINESS

In addition to leading trips in The Footsteps of Jesus, we now also lead trips through Turkey and Greece in The Footsteps of Paul. We find the same thing is true almost everywhere we go in the Middle East. Extended families share life and work together in family businesses. In restaurants, shops, hotels, and transportation enterprises, we find grandparents, parents, siblings, in-laws, and cousins all working together for a common purpose. The reasons for this haven't changed since biblical times. When you live and work together, you have more resources to face and overcome the inevitable challenges life throws at you. You can provide for and protect your family more effectively that way. Jesus' family could do better in the building business by working together as an *oikos*. Simon and Andrew's families could do better by developing a fishing business together and building a partnership with the *oikos* of Zebedee and his sons James and John.

By working together, the extended family of Simon and Andrew, along with that of James and John, had built successful family businesses that afforded them the opportunity to live with financial security in large homes in some of the most sought after neighborhoods of their town. Imagine their surprise when Jesus offered to take their *oikos* businesses to a whole new level! Luke tells us that, after borrowing Simon's fishing boat to use as a floating pulpit, Jesus gave these professional fishermen some free advice: *"Put out into the deep and let down your nets for a catch."* After hauling in a net-splitting catch of a lifetime, Simon fell down before Jesus in amazement, and then Jesus made a unique family business proposition: *"'Do not be afraid; from now on you will be catching men.' And when they had brought their boats to land, they left everything and followed him."* (Luke 5:1-11)

Jesus entered into the *oikos* of Simon and Andrew and showed them how to build a whole new kind of family by opening the door and inviting in the outcasts and the broken. Now he was telling these fishermen this new kind of family was going to develop a new kind of business by going out after a new catch. No longer would they simply be going after fish; now finding lost people was going to be their goal. Later in his ministry, when Jesus entered the *oikos* of a tax collector named Zacchaeus and transformed his family business, Jesus was crystal clear about the purpose of his mission: *"For the Son of Man came to seek and to save the lost."* (Luke 19:10) Jesus was showing us how to move a family beyond self-serving protection and provision into a purpose far greater than itself.

This takes us back to Caesarea Philippi when Jesus gave Simon his new name. It is no coincidence that a man from an extended family of stonemasons and builders gave his key disciple the name *Rocky* and invited him to be part of the greatest building project of all time. The purpose of every Kingdom-oriented family is to find people who are far from God and show them how they can become a part of the Father's family on mission. Jesus entered Simon's family and transformed their fishing business into a Kingdom business. Now Jesus was telling Simon Peter the time had come for his family to join in the heavenly Father's family business and be part of building the Kingdom of God.

WHAT KIND OF FAMILY?

When Pam and I were engaged, we did premarital counseling with the pastor I had grown up with. Knowing my workaholic tendencies, he wisely warned us about the dangers of allowing ministry to negatively impact our marriage and family life. In spite of the potential dangers, we knew God was not calling us to choose between family or mission. Our desire was to do both well. We believed God was calling us to build a strong marriage and healthy family while at the same time building a healthy, Kingdom-advancing church. The problem was that these goals often seemed at odds with each other. We were part of larger staff-led, programmatic churches where there was a lot going on all the time, creating a constant pull for me to do more and spend more time at church. As a result Pam developed a strong firewall between our home and our ministry to make sure I was spending enough time with her and our boys. I tried to avoid bringing work home by not talking much about church-related topics when we were together as a couple or a family.

While these steps helped to protect our family from being overwhelmed by the demands of a busy, programmatic ministry, it had other unwanted effects. By compartmentalizing our lives into family and mission, Pam and I ended up feeling pulled in two different directions. Resentment tended to accumulate in both directions. Although Pam had always been an active leader in the church, she found herself more focused on family, while I was more focused on our mission. These two callings always seemed to drive us apart rather than bring us together. Whenever we would achieve what seemed like a good balance, it only took one unexpected challenge to knock us off balance and pit our mission against our family once again.

> Jesus entered Simon's family and transformed their fishing business into a Kingdom business. Now Jesus was telling Simon Peter the time had come for his family to join in the heavenly Father's family business and be part of building the Kingdom of God.

As we began this journey into Jesus-shaped discipleship, Pam and I noticed something very different about the families of the people from whom we were learning. We noticed their lives did not seem to be compartmentalized the way ours was. There was a natural integration we had not seen before. They didn't have one way of being a family and another way of carrying out their mission. They didn't seem pulled in different directions trying to keep both these balls in the air at the same time. They weren't trying to walk the tightrope of balance by guarding their boundaries. Instead they had healthy rhythms of rest and work that resulted in good fruit. They had strong marriages and healthy kids, but were also highly effective in carrying out their mission. They weren't perfect, but we liked their way of life better than ours.

Gradually we began to emulate this way of life and learn how to integrate our lives rather than compartmentalize. Instead of setting up a firewall between our family and our mission, we began to see our family was meant to be at the heart of our mission. Instead of constantly trying to achieve a fragile balance, we learned healthier rhythms that built up momentum that could be maintained even when the unexpected happened. We have come to understand we don't have to choose between family OR mission. We don't have to try to balance family AND mission. Instead, we are learning how to become a family ON mission.

family **OR** mission

family **AND** mission

family **ON** mission

The more we embraced God's family as our family, the more we realized we also had a family business—a Kingdom business. Our family does not exist solely for its own sake. Our family exists for a bigger purpose—as much bigger as people are more valuable than fish! Now we see our family business as the mission of God. It is not another compartment we have to try and fit into our already busy lives—it is at the heart of everything we do. Our mission is not just a mission with our biological, nuclear family, but also a mission with the extended spiritual family we are building.

PUTTING IDEAS INTO ACTION

Jesus said those who hear his word and act on it are like the wise man who built his *oikos* on the rock. So we began to act in faith on the things we felt Jesus was saying to us. The first thing we did was to begin growing our nuclear family into an extended family. For most of our married life, our home was somewhat of a fortress—a place to retreat from the pressures of ministry. Now we began to open the doors of our home, and our lives, and invite people in. We started with the people we were discipling. We began spending time with them outside our scheduled Huddle times and just started having fun together. We invited them to bring their spouses and kids along.

We kept things lightweight and low-maintenance so it didn't put undue stress on anyone. We started gathering every other Sunday after church to build a stronger sense of extended family. Everyone brought food to share, and we spent some time sharing encouragement and praying together. We slowly learned to integrate these folks into some of the regular activities of our family. If we were going to the movies or to the beach or out to dinner, we included those who were becoming part of our extended spiritual family. It didn't happen overnight, but by listening to God, following the example

> The more we embraced God's family as our family, the more we realized we also had a family business—a Kingdom business. Our family does not exist solely for its own sake. Our family exists for a bigger purpose—as much bigger as people are more valuable than fish! Now we see our family business as the mission of God.

of those who were mentoring us, and being accountable to concrete steps of faith, gradually we developed our own *oikos*.

The next step was to identify our Kingdom family business. There were many needs and countless unreached people in our community, but we knew we needed to seek and follow Jesus' leading. We had lived in the same neighborhood for about twelve years, but the only neighbors we knew were those who went to our church. I was deeply convicted that I had been ignoring the lost people in my own neighborhood. God showed us our mission field was the block we lived on. We began to make room in our lives to befriend our neighbors. We started spending more time in our front yard, and not just the backyard. We took the initiative to introduce ourselves and strike up conversations. We looked for ways to serve those on our block and became better neighbors to them. I started babysitting for one over-worked couple a few doors down. We invited three couples that seemed to be receptive and positive People of Peace over for dinner. Pretty soon we got invitations to several of their kids' birthday parties. My sons and I organized some men's poker nights at our house. Before long we noticed neighbors going out of their way to talk with us and even serve us.

As we built relationships with our neighbors who were not people of faith or active in a faith community, we then began to connect them with our growing spiritual family. We walked our neighborhood in prayer, listening to what God was saying to us about serving and reaching our neighbors. About once a month we started planning events we thought our unbelieving or unchurched neighbors and friends would enjoy. At Christmastime we baked cookies and delivered them to neighbors while caroling just to let them know we cared. In the summer we gathered for picnics in the nearby park and organized simple games for the kids. We gathered items for a yard sale and gave the proceeds to a family in the neighborhood that was struggling with medical bills. We looked for any way we could serve our neighbors and invite them into our new spiritual family.

As Pam and I began to learn discipleship and mission as a way of life, we were disappointed we hadn't been exposed to these things earlier in life when our sons were younger. They were in their late teens and early twenties when we began building an extended family on mission, and we assumed it was too late for them share this new missional way of life with us. However, to our surprise they both seemed drawn to our emerging patterns and lifestyle. Although they both were moving into increasing independence in college and marriage, they began to orbit back into our lives more closely than they had in years. Our older son's wife, our younger son's girlfriend, and their peers often came with them and joined in with our extended family on mission. In a very organic way, we found ourselves sharing a new sense of being a family on mission with our sons and those who were connected with them in spite of being in the launching years. We discovered that no matter what stage of life you are in, or whether your biological family embraces this direction (remember Jesus' rejection by his own family), it is never too late to learn how to live as a family on mission.

We didn't see massive conversions or immediate revival break out in our neighborhood, but in time we saw lives changed by the power of God's love working through an extended spiritual family on mission together. We noticed the tenor of our neighborhood changing. People were more open and engaging with each other. We had opportunities to make a practical difference in the lives of people who really needed help. Over the course of a couple of years, we saw a number of people come to faith in Jesus, and some of them ended up joining our church. Some connected with other churches. The Kingdom of God was extended. We challenged and equipped the people we were discipling to start building their own extended families on mission, and a number of them did. Some of them identified other Kingdom family businesses, and their mission took them to different places in our community where they began to serve and reach different kinds of people. It was so exciting and fulfilling to see those we were discipling begin to disciple others and build spiritual families that were seeking and saving the lost.

YOUR FAMILY ON MISSION

Maybe, in answering Jesus' call to mission, you have tried desperately to balance your family and your mission. Or maybe you have felt the tension of choosing between having a family or fulfilling your mission. The Good News is Jesus offers us a better way. It's not that we need to balance our family and our mission—rather we need to learn how to integrate our family and our mission into one. Not two things, but one thing. As Sally Breen likes to say, "God has given us one life to live, so live one life!"[25] If you are drawn to the vision in this book for empowering missional disciples, it begins with learning how to build a family on mission.

---

25. Mike and Sally Breen, *Family on Mission* (Pawley's Island: 3DM Publishing, 2014). This is a wonderfully practical book on how to build a family on mission. After finishing this book, reading *Family on Mission* with those you consider family is a great next step on this journey.

18

A FRUITFUL RHYTHM

NOT ENOUGH ROOM!

When some people first hear about building a family on mission, they feel overwhelmed by all of it. Their schedule is already so full that they can't imagine inviting more people into their life and their home. Some people, particularly those who are naturally introverted, are afraid all their energy will be drained by being around groups of people all the time. To them, integrating family with mission can sound like boundary violations of the worst kind.

It is critical for us to remember how good our Father is and that he always wants what is good for us. When we see Jesus calling us to follow his example, it is because his way is the best possible way for us. Jesus will not lead us into something that is bad for us. He certainly warned us of the cost of following him and never promised it would be easy, but as we learn to die to our old self and take up our cross, the abundant life he promised is the fruit of walking as he walked.

When we look at Jesus' life, we can see he lived with very intentional and healthy rhythms. Early in the morning, while it was still dark, he withdrew to a lonely place to spend time alone with his heavenly Father. From that place of abiding and rest, Jesus then stepped into the busy, fruitful life of ministry he was living. Every Sabbath day Jesus gathered with others at the synagogue for worship and rest with his extended family. This wasn't a burdensome, legalistic observance, but an intentional time for restoration and renewal.

After some days of healing the sick and declaring the Good News of the Kingdom, Jesus took his disciples away to a peaceful place to rest for a while. Even when this time of rest was interrupted by crowds seeking Jesus, these healthy rhythms allowed them enough margin that they didn't have to send the crowds away. They were rested enough to have compassion on shepherdless sheep. Once in a while, Jesus took the disciples away on a longer retreat, to an area where no one would even recognize them, so they could have an extended period of rest. Again, even when a time like this was interrupted by a pagan woman seeking healing for her son, Jesus was able to respond positively to her profound faith.

As Jesus' renown grew, he experienced tremendous pressure to perform and had countless demands on his time, but it did not overwhelm him. Because Jesus lived with these intentional rhythms of rest and work, he was able to respond appropriately to the needs of so many, yet still maintain a healthy lifestyle. Jesus was setting a clear pattern for his disciples to follow. He is calling us to follow him in that pattern as well.

THE VINE AND THE BRANCHES

On the last night Jesus was with the disciples before his crucifixion, he made a special point of sharing the Passover meal with them in a secret upper room in Jerusalem. After the dinner, as they were walking north through the Kidron Valley toward the olive grove called Gethsemane at the base of the Mount of Olives, Jesus drew an amazing picture for the disciples and for us. Probably pointing to vineyards that grew along the slope

beside them, Jesus told the disciples he was like the main trunk of a grapevine. He told them what everyone in that culture knew— branches that bear no fruit get cut off and thrown into the fire. In contrast he pointed out how branches that do bear fruit get pruned in order that they might bear more fruit. Then he said, *"I am the vine; you are the branches. Whoever abides in me and I in him, he it is that bears much fruit, for apart from me you can do nothing."* (John 15:5)

Jesus is comparing the connection between the grapevine and its branches with the Covenantal relationship that makes us one with him. Just as the main trunk of the vine provides everything the branch needs to grow and become fruitful, so we are dependent for Jesus to provide everything we need to live the abundant and fruitful life for which we are created. The crucial factor in living that abundant life is the connection between us and Jesus. If the branch is not deeply woven into the fiber of the vine, it will not receive the nutrients it needs to flourish and become fruitful. On the other hand, if that branch stays connected to the vine, it will naturally grow and produce good fruit. Jesus says the same is true of us. Everything depends on nurturing our connection with Jesus.

> If the branch is not deeply woven into the fiber of the vine, it will not receive the nutrients it needs to flourish and become fruitful. On the other hand, if that branch stays connected to the vine, it will naturally grow and produce good fruit.

The word translated *abide* in this passage is the Greek word *meno*, which means literally to stay in one place, to remain, to dwell somewhere. At the Passover meal that night Jesus told the disciples he was fulfilling God's promise to make a New Covenant with his people, a Covenant that makes oneness with him possible. When Jesus died and rose from the dead, he completed that Covenant for us. Now by God's grace, through faith in Jesus, we are united with him in this New Covenant through his blood. In this passage Jesus is telling us, unlike literal branches, we can choose to abide in that Covenantal connection with him, or we can choose to operate apart from him. If we choose to operate independently of him, our lives will not produce good fruit that lasts. As we learn to remain and rest in his presence, lasting good fruit will naturally be produced in our lives.

This is the secret of Jesus' extraordinary life. He knew how to abide in the Father's love so that the good fruit of the Kingdom naturally flowed from his life. When Jesus withdrew early in the mornings, he spent time alone with his heavenly Father. When Jesus took a weekly day of rest and worshiped at the synagogue, he was abiding with the community. When Jesus took his disciples away on retreats locally or out of the area, he was abiding with his closest friends. Jesus intentionally developed rhythms that nurtured his connection with the Father and his spiritual family. The result was that his life produced incredible amounts of eternal Kingdom fruit. When Jesus calls us to follow him, he is calling us to live in these same rhythms of abiding and bearing fruit.

LEARNING JESUS' RHYTHMS

Pam and I have always struggled with the busy pace of life and ministry. Once we were around people who intentionally lived according to the rhythms of Jesus, we saw how much better it was than always trying to police boundaries and seek some kind of elusive balance. The people who were discipling us had a daily rhythm of reading the Scriptures and praying, both by themselves and as a family. They also scheduled intentional days and seasons for abiding and rest. Out of these times of abiding, they moved into fruitful Kingdom work. They described it as a rhythm of swinging from rest and abiding, into work and fruitfulness and then back again.

Gradually Pam and I started developing these same rhythms in our lives. Instead of reading Scripture on our own separate plans, we decided to get on the same Bible reading plan. We started listening to a daily devotional online based on those same Scripture readings. As a result we both became a lot more consistent in spending time with the Father each day, because we could support each other in establishing that daily rhythm. We also found we started to share with each other and pray together more regularly about what God was saying to us and what we felt he wanted us to do. Now we find that reading God's Word and praying about it together is as natural each morning as eating breakfast.

We began to seek healthier rhythms in other areas of our lives as well. Jesus said fruitful branches are the ones the vine grower prunes back so they will produce more and better fruit. So we began to submit to the Father's pruning in our lives, allowing him to clean out some of the things that were good but not necessary to make room for the new things he wanted to do. We found this allowed us more time to disciple leaders, invite people into our lives, and learn how to live a missional life in our neighborhood.

We also started to practice a full 24-hour Sabbath day each week. From

Friday night until Saturday night, we only do things we want to do. We go out on Friday night. Sleep in on Saturday morning. Have breakfast in our pajamas. I might go surfing. Pam might putter in the garden. We might sit out on the patio reading books or the Bible, or take a walk or visit friends. We get to do whatever helps us rest, recharge, and reconnect with the Father and one another. I found myself looking forward to and excited about our weekly days of rest!

We began to look at our calendar differently. Instead of just scheduling things however they came up, we planned periods of rest to enjoy in between the busy periods of fruitful activity we knew God was calling us to. Sometimes these abiding seasons include times to get away for a weekend or a longer vacation, but they also come with a mindset that we are making more room for rest and abiding during those times. These restful seasons increase our capacity to engage in fruitful activity with greater effectiveness and joy.

Today this rhythm of abiding and fruitfulness comes much more naturally for us. We still have to be intentional about protecting time each day, each week, seasonally, and annually to rest and reconnect, but it is no longer difficult because it has become a way of life for us. Momentum builds when you establish these kinds of rhythms in your life. Even when unexpected things get thrown your way, it doesn't keep you from swinging right back into those rhythms. When we were trying to maintain boundaries and balance, I always felt like I was walking on a tightrope, and the littlest thing could come along and knock me off. Now the rhythm of Jesus' life of abiding and bearing fruit is like a flywheel that keeps us following in his footsteps no matter what comes our way.

A PICTURE OF HEALTHY RHYTHMS

Just as Jesus used visual images familiar to the people of his time, such as lilies of the field and birds of the air, we use images that help people in our day remember, practice, and pass on the principles Jesus taught and modeled for his disciples. We envision the rhythms of Jesus' life as a semicircle, the shape scribed by a pendulum swinging back and forth from one side to the other[26]:

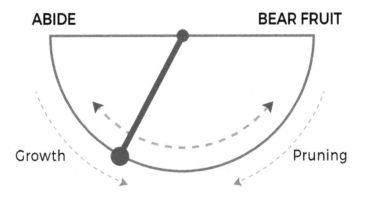

The Semicircle LifeShape gives us a picture of Jesus' rhythm of swinging from restful abiding into fruitful work and then back again on a daily, weekly, seasonal, and annual basis. It also reminds us that when we get stuck over in fruitful work too long and can't seem to get back to abiding, we need to submit to the Father's pruning. Likewise, when we have spent enough time abiding, the natural result is growth leading to more and better fruitfulness.

This is an incredibly important tool for those of us who live in the modern Western world where life is moving so fast and we are constantly under pressure to add more and more and more to our already full lives. We are bombarded with the message that more is always better whereas Jesus

---

26. Breen, *Building a Discipling Culture*, p. 85ff.

shows us in the Kingdom of God, less is actually more. He said, *"For who-ever would save his life will lose it, but whoever loses his life for my sake will save it."* (Luke 9:24) Submitting to the Father's pruning is a way of losing our old life so we might step into more of the new life God has in mind for us.

Families on mission make intentional space for abiding on a daily, weekly, seasonal, and annual basis. You will find healthy rhythms are what make a discipling way of life possible and are essential to sustaining the fruitful-ness of a missional *oikos*. We found the process of pruning and establish-ing healthy rhythms gave us time to invest in people's lives, invite them into our family, and we still had more time for rest and renewal. Using Jesus' language of abiding, pruning, and bearing fruit along with this picture of the pendulum swinging consistently between Covenantal rest and Kingdom work is essential in developing a discipling culture where people are learning how to live as missional families.

> We are bombarded with the message that more is always better whereas Jesus shows us in the Kingdom of God, less is actually more.

19

A VEHICLE FOR MISSIONAL FAMILY

THE BIRTH OF A MISSIONAL MOVEMENT

When Mike Breen was called to lead St. Thomas' Church in Sheffield, England, in 1994, he began to develop the discipling language and strategies we have been describing in this book. It was an active church with many small groups that were great for building community (IN), but not many people were actively engaging with those outside the church (OUT). Realizing the Personal Space of a small group was too intimidating for new people, Mike challenged the leaders of small groups to combine their groups once a month with at least two other small groups to form a mid-sized group of people, gathering in what we have called Social Space.

These Clusters, as they were first called, focused on activities designed to help them connect with people outside the church. The Clusters met outside the church in homes, pubs, parks, or other neutral spaces, usually around a shared meal. Some Clusters formed around common interests like hiking, sports, or workplace issues. Others formed on a geographical basis in neighborhoods or on school campuses. Each Cluster started to take on a unique sense of identity and calling as it clarified who it was called to serve and reach.

Because the Clusters were larger than a small group, they had more resources and courage to move out of their comfort zone and engage in mission together. The larger size also made it more comfortable for new people to join them, because they didn't feel put on the spot the way they would in the more personal environment of a small group. Although the Clusters were large enough to be less intimidating, they were still small enough for new people to get connected and feel a part of the community. I call this the *Goldilocks Principle*–the mid-sized group is *just right* to reach new people!

Because the church had been developing a discipling culture through Huddles, the number of spiritual leaders was growing in the congregation and in the Clusters, which enabled them to multiply new Clusters. As the Clusters multiplied, each with a different missional focus, they were able to relate to and connect with an incredible variety of people in their large, diverse city.

Over time these Clusters became the primary vehicle of a missional movement, fueled by a growing ability to exercise Jesus' authority and guided by a desire to seek and save the lost. They were led by discipling leaders who were intentionally training others to multiply the mission by doing the same with their disciples in new neighborhoods and networks. In a city where less than 2 percent of the population attended a church service on a given Sunday, St. Thomas' Church became the fastest growing and largest church, not only in England, but eventually in all of Europe.

The most remarkable thing about this statistic is that it did not just represent crowds of people gathering in large worship gatherings led by a charismatic leader. It represented a network of extended spiritual families making disciples and living out the mission of Jesus in every nook and cranny of Sheffield. Rather than keeping track of worship attendance, they focused on how many people were in intentional discipling relationships and how many were part of extended families on mission. This vehicle began to spread to other churches in the UK and Europe and eventually started to be called Missional Communities.

Two things happened to demonstrate that the culture of empowering missional discipleship at St. Thomas' was producing something very different than the typical megachurch. First was the loss of their building. Their Sunday worship gatherings had outgrown the traditional stone building where the church started, so they had moved into the city center and were worshiping in a large nightclub. Out of the blue, the fire marshal declared the building unsafe for large gatherings, and they were evicted. With no other viable options for large worship gatherings, the church began worshiping in the various mid-sized Missional Communities that met around the city. Amazingly, St. Thomas' Church didn't shrink numerically during this period—it actually grew even faster!

The second thing that happened was that, after just ten years of leading St. Thomas', Mike and Sally Breen discerned God calling them to leave England and move their extended spiritual family to the United States. One of the greatest challenges a megachurch faces is how to replace its primary leader. Mike stepped down from leadership at St. Thomas' at what seemed to be the peak of its development and turned over leadership to a young, untested leader he had discipled named Paul Maconochie. After a year of transition, the church began to grow in making disciples and reaching the lost at an even greater rate under Paul's leadership. It was evident what was happening at St. Thomas' was not about Mike—it was about the development of an empowered discipling culture that was leading a movement of extended families on mission.

A few years ago, Pam and I were in Sheffield for a gathering of church leaders at St. Thomas' Church, and we took part in a bus tour of the city hosted by two of their pastors. Using a microphone, they narrated as we drove around the city, describing some of the hundreds of Missional Communities (MCs) planted in the many different kinds of neighborhoods of Sheffield. As we drove through an upper-class neighborhood of stately stone mansions, they told us of MCs that reached out to the wealthy residents of that area by hosting wine and cheese parties. As we passed through the university district, they pointed out the pubs where MCs met at 2 AM after closing time to reach students. Driving through an area populated predominately by poorer Muslim immigrants, they explained how a number of families had sold their homes and moved into that neighborhood to establish an MC that focused on incarnating the love of Jesus to their neighbors.

This missional tour of Sheffield went on and on for nearly two hours, as we heard about the work of hundreds of extended families on mission in a city where 98 percent of the population desperately need to meet people who are following Jesus. Sitting on that bus, Pam and I were amazed to see how empowered disciples were reaching out to their entire city by learning to live as extended families on mission.

IN NEED OF TRAINING WHEELS

I vividly remember the Christmas morning I watched my oldest son, Bobby, pedal off on his first two-wheeled bicycle. He had mastered the stable trike, but now it was time for the freedom and thrill of two wheels. Or, almost time. While assembling the bike, I was sure to bolt two training wheels on his back axle. You know how they work. These smaller wheels ride just a little higher than the back tire. As the bike tips one way or the other, the training wheels help stabilize it and keep it upright. I ran alongside him at first, helping him get the feel, but now he was on his own. As Bobby rode out into the great expanse of our cul-de-sac, I saw him begin to tip to the left, but then the left training wheel caught him and pushed him back to the right. He held the line for a couple more pedals, then the bike lurched to the other side, but the right training wheel did its job and kept him from crashing and burning.

It is a great thing to have training wheels in place when you are learning a skill as tricky as riding a bike. The same is true when we are learning something as challenging as building a missional family. In Jesus' time no one needed to learn how to live as an *oikos*, because that was the naturally inherited way of life. In our culture we have largely lost the memory of extended family, so we have a lot to learn if we are going to follow the way of Jesus. Most of us don't know how to build a family business, so embracing the Father's Kingdom business in our family will take some training. We need enough structure in place so we can learn what it looks like to do mission as an extended family in our context, but enough freedom so we can grow into an authentic missional *oikos* and not just another kind of church program. We need a set of training wheels just far enough off the ground so we can try out this missional way of life without crashing and burning.

A Missional Community is meant to be our training wheels, helping us learn how to live as an extended spiritual family on mission together. An MC is a mid-sized group of people who are living UP-IN-OUT lives together. They have a Covenant commitment to one another as a spiritual family and a Kingdom calling from God to serve and reach the lost. They spend time together learning how to listen to God, building one another up in love, and seeking to connect with those who are far from God. An MC is larger than a small group and smaller than a worship service. We like to say they are small enough to care, but large enough to dare. They normally meet outside the church, gather around meals, and have a clearly defined focus for their mission. They have discipling culture at their core and are designed to multiply as disciples grow in their faith and skills to lead others.[27] Simply put, a Missional Community is a houseful of friends on a mission.

As I explained in Chapter Ten, a Huddle is not discipleship, but rather a vehicle to help us learn how to build and multiply discipling relationships. In the same way, an MC is not a family on mission, but a vehicle with training wheels to help us learn this missional way of life with others. An MC provides the organizational structure to help us grow organically into missional *oikos*. Eventually, as discipleship and mission in an extended family becomes our natural way of life, the training wheels of MC can come off, and we will simply be living in and multiplying families on mission.

NOT JUST A FAD

An MC is a mid-sized group of people who are living UP-IN-OUT lives together. They have a Covenant commitment to one another as a spiritual family and a Kingdom calling from God to serve and reach the lost. They spend time together learning how to listen to God, building one another up in love, and seeking to connect with those who are far from God.

Missional Communities have become one of the latest buzzwords in the current missional movement. Among church leaders who are seeking new ways to extend God's Kingdom, everyone seems to be talking about MCs. It is encouraging that so many people are talking about how to regain the missional focus of Jesus' movement. The danger is that MCs will become another quick-fix ministry fad that disappears as quickly as it came when people are attracted to the next new trend. In truth, MCs are an expression of the way Jesus and the early church

27. For more information on Missional Communities see Mike Breen, *Leading Missional Communities* (Pawley's Island: 3DM Publishing, 2013).

changed the world, so this is not meant to be a fad or trend, but a way of life that becomes deeply rooted in our identity and calling as a family on mission.

Jesus told his disciples in the upper room, *"I am the way, and the truth, and the life"* (John 14:6). Most followers of Jesus have rightly focused on the truth of Jesus; the words he spoke and the words written about him in the Bible. In the last hundred years there has been a renewed interest in the life of Jesus and learning how to do the kinds of works he did. But curiously, many seem to have forgotten about pursuing the way of Jesus, the actual patterns and rhythms of his life. As we have seen, at the time of Constantine the church largely took on the ways of Roman society rather than the way of Jesus. Ironically, the first name given to the movement Jesus began was "The Way"! (Acts 9:2; 19:9, 23; 22:4; 24:14, 22) Our movement today is primarily about relearning how to live more fully in the Way of Jesus, so we will be empowered to speak the Word of Jesus and carry out the Works of Jesus with greater fruitfulness. We can picture it this way:

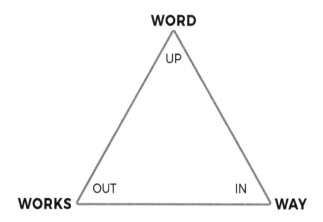

The reason we are investing in a vehicle like MCs is that we want to learn how to live the Way Jesus did, as an extended spiritual family on mission together. One of the problems with the current popularity of MCs is that people embrace the shiny new vehicle, but miss that it is meant to teach us to live more fully in the Way of Jesus. Jesus built a discipling culture which was at the heart of his extended missional family. Many people today are excited about MCs, but are missing the role of empowered discipleship in fulfilling their mission.

When MCs are expressed as the next church growth program, it completely misses the point that this is meant to develop as an authentic extended spiritual family. When MCs are formed before leaders have begun to develop a discipling culture, there is very little leadership capital to multiply the movement. If the leaders of MCs don't know how to operate in Jesus' authority and power and pass that on to others, there will not be enough strength to overcome the inevitable spiritual and worldly opposition they will face. It is like building a car without an engine. It looks good, and people can get inside, but pretty soon they get tired of pushing the car, so they abandon it. Missional Communities without discipling culture and biblical empowerment at their core will soon wither and fade away with little lasting fruit.

When I first got involved in this movement, I was very excited about the potential it had to bring greater fruitfulness to the church I was leading. This excitement led me to move too quickly into the implementation of MCs. We had started some Huddles, but most of our Huddles had not yet multiplied to the next generation of disciple-making. When I began casting the vision for MCs, a number of leaders we were Huddling stepped forward to start new MCs, but most of them had not started discipling others. We made a big public launch of seven MCs, which was exciting, but none of them had a Huddle of leaders at their core who could train others to operate in Jesus' authority and power. As a result, many of the leaders of the new Missional Communities became discouraged because they couldn't get others to help with the leadership. Most people in the MCs said that they were too busy to help lead or that they did not consider themselves leaders. Before long several of the initial leaders burned out and gave up on Missional Communities.

The mistake we made was launching Missional Communities as if they were a church program which only fed the consumeristic culture our programmatic approach had already produced. Eventually I had to learn how to build a family on mission myself so I could disciple other people into the way of life that I was learning. We need to be able to show people what this looks like, not just talk about it. This took far longer than our big splashy MC launch, but the fruit of it was so much better. Unless you as a leader are willing to grow into this as a way of life with your own biological and spiritual family, you will not be very successful training and empowering others to do it. Unless they have a living example to follow, it will be difficult for them to learn this missional way of life and pass it on to others. Unless you are willing to give it enough time to put down roots and grow organically, it will not be a sustainable movement that bears lasting fruit. For those who are willing to open up their lives, learn from the examples of others, and invest the time and commitment it takes to develop a genuine family on mission, MCs are an invaluable vehicle to help us learn a way of life that looks more like Jesus' life.

EVERYBODY GETS TO PLAY

As I explained earlier, in biblical times extended families were built around a family business in which everyone played a part. If it was an *oikos* of shepherds, some members of the family would herd the sheep and goats, some would milk them, some would tend to their health, some would shear them, some would bundle and transport the wool, some would spin wool into yarn, some would weave garments, etc. Everyone played a critical role in the success of the family business. The same is true of the family on mission.

One of the great things about Missional Communities is they provide an environment where everyone gets to participate in the life and mission of the Body of Christ. Too often, in our typical church gatherings, only those with certain skills or knowledge get to take an active part in the spiritual life of the community. The singers sing, the readers read, the preachers preach, the prayers pray, and the announcers announce. Most of us are left on the sidelines watching. In contrast to this, Paul described the church as a human body and emphasized how every part is critical to the health of the whole. He specified five critical roles within the body that help us grow up into the fullness of Christ and strengthen his Body, the Church. When writing to churches in Asia Minor Paul said, *"But grace was given to each one of us according to the measure of Christ's gift... And he gave the apostles, the prophets, the evangelists, the shepherds and teachers, to equip the saints for the work of ministry, for building up the body of Christ."* (Ephesians 4:7, 11-12)

In an MC there are opportunities for everyone to grow in their gifting as they learn to serve and lead. Everyone gets to grow as a servant by bringing food to share, serving the meals, and helping to clean up afterward. Everyone gets to grow as an apostle as we discern the new ways God is calling us to fulfill our unique missional calling. Everyone gets to grow as a prophet when we spend time listening for what God is saying and sharing encouraging words and pictures with each other. Everyone gets to grow as an evangelist when we go out and find ways to connect with our People of Peace. Everyone gets to grow as a shepherd when we pray for each other and comfort those who are hurting in our midst. Everyone gets to grow as a teacher when we discuss God's Word and how to put it into practice.

Not only are there roles for everyone, but there is a place for every kind of person in an MC. Jesus specifically chose twelve men to be part of his inner circle of disciples, but he opened the door of the *oikos* in Capernaum to everyone who would come—even the demon-possessed! Huddles are a vehicle for discipling leaders and, as such, only certain people are invited into a given Huddle. However, everyone is invited into an MC. There is a place for people who know nothing about Jesus or the Bible, as well as those who

> Unless you as a leader are willing to grow into this as a way of life with your own biological and spiritual family, you will not be very successful training and empowering others to do it.

have been walking with Jesus their entire lives. There is a place for men and women of every kind of background, economic status, racial heritage, educational level, and vocational identity. MCs are healthiest when they are multigenerational, just like an extended family. There is a place for older people, younger people, babies, parents, teens, middle-aged people, and everyone in between. MCs are great fun because everyone gets to play.

MISSIONAL RHYTHMS

Just as Jesus demonstrates a healthy rhythm of abiding and bearing fruit, he also shows us how to live in healthy three-dimensional rhythms of UP, IN, and OUT.

UP   Jesus was always in close communion with his heavenly Father. He simply did what he saw the Father doing and spoke the words the Father gave him to speak.

IN   Sometimes Jesus focused on his relationship with the twelve disciples. He took them away by themselves for times of teaching, training, and abiding.

OUT   Other times Jesus focused on their mission. He welcomed the outcast into their *oikos* in Capernaum and healed the broken. He took the houseful of disciples out on the highways and byways to seek and save the lost.

As we learn how to build missional families, it is important to develop the same kind of rhythms in our Missional Communities.

Practically, this means Jesus-shaped MCs will establish a regular rhythm of gatherings that focus on UP and IN along with regular activities that focus on IN and OUT. For instance, our MC typically gathers every other Sunday over lunch for an UP-IN time together. Everyone brings food to share, and after eating we share encouraging testimonies of the good things God is doing in our lives. Then we open it up for people to share some things God has been saying to them through their daily Bible reading. Then we break into groups of three to share personal prayer requests and pray for each other. This is a typical UP-IN time together.

About once a month we plan an IN-OUT activity aimed at helping our unbelieving or unchurched friends connect with our spiritual family. This could be as simple as a prayer walk in the neighborhood or hanging out in the front yard to meet people who are out and about. It could be going out to do random acts of kindness, like giving out water bottles or doing neighborhood cleanup or yard work. It could be raising money for those in need or offering practical support to someone who is struggling. It could be organizing a public event like a picnic and games in the park where everyone is invited. It could be a gathering in someone's home and inviting People of Peace to come and join in the fun. The point of these IN-OUT activities is to find a way to identify those who are open to us, so we can begin to build relationships with them, so they can encounter Jesus.

One helpful strategy in establishing the rhythms of a Missional Community is to look at the existing patterns of your lives and discern the opportunities for community and mission they offer. If you currently attend your children's soccer games twice a week, how can you leverage those opportunities to find People of Peace? If you already organize an annual mission trip to serve the poor in Mexico, how can your Missional Community take advantage of that event to further your mission? If summer camping trips are the normal pattern of your life, what are the opportunities there to coordinate and build deeper relationships within your Missional Community?

Building a spiritual family that follows the example of Jesus also means there will be seasons when the MC takes some time off from their regular gatherings before resuming a normal schedule again. Our MCs typically take three-to-four-week breaks in the summer, over Christmas and New Year's, and during the Easter holiday. These down times give the leaders an opportunity to rest and abide, and give space for vacations and holiday activities and are critical rhythms for a healthy family on mission to produce good fruit that lasts. This doesn't mean we don't get together and enjoy sharing life together. It just means we take a break from the more organized expressions of our missional family. The point of living as part of a Missional Community is not to make our lives more stressful, but more fruitful. There are sacrifices and challenging steps of faith we are called to make on this journey of building a family on mission. But when we remember that in God's Kingdom less can be more, it leads us into a more abundant life.

20

GOD'S PLAN TO SAVE THE WORLD

THE DIGITAL REVOLUTION

Whether you love it or you hate it, the truth is that digital devices have profoundly changed the way we live. With the development of the personal computer and the establishment of the internet, the die was cast for the simple binary code of 1s and 0s to start a revolution. Today we hold in our hand or wear on our wrist computers more powerful than those that sat on our desks twenty years ago.

Everyone is affected by this revolution. I used to read newspapers and watch the news on television. Now I check the daily news summary from the New York Times on my phone in the morning and get up-to-the-minute notices from various agencies on breaking news throughout the day. I used to pore over maps before taking a trip into new territory. Now I click on the address a friend has texted me, and my navigation program automatically loads the turn-by-turn directions and reads them to me as I travel. I used to have shelves and shelves of books double deep. Now I carry my entire library and do all my reading on a handheld tablet.

I'm no computer expert, but I love the tools the digital age has made possible. From a layperson's point of view, it all works on the basis of four primary components: the programming language, the operating system, a graphical user interface (GUI), and killer apps:

> **1. Programming Language:** This is how the simple on/off switch of digital 1s and 0s is translated into something meaningful. It's sort of like the way the various sounds we make with our mouth get turned into meaningful sentences. The key to a device's power is the strength of its programming language. The programming language ultimately determines how much our device can handle. The reason Apple surged to the forefront of the personal digital device revolution in the 1990s is not just because their products looked so cool wrapped in brushed aluminum, but because Steve Jobs used the most powerful language available to write his new operating system, OSX.

> **2. Operating System (OS):** The OS uses the programming language to tell your device what to do and how to operate. When you turn your device on and a swirling image appears with a distinctive theme song playing in the background, that is your OS at work. When you touch an image and right click or left click or double click, the operating system tells your device what to do. When you open an

application, it runs because your operating system connects the program to your device. It is kind of like the plumbing system in a building that gets water everywhere it needs to be. Everything your device does for you works through the operating system.

3. Graphical User Interface (GUI): This is the collection of icons on the screen that allow you to interact with your device without having to know complex programming code. I vividly remember visiting my wife's office in 1987 and watching her work on a brand new Macintosh Computer. I was amazed that she didn't need to type in various DOS prompts. She simply clicked on the picture of a file folder, and it automatically opened to a collection of documents. Then she clicked on a picture of a piece of paper, and it opened a document she had been working on. GUIs are what make the power of computing available to everyone. You don't need to know an esoteric code to get your device to do what you want it to do— you just start touching pictures, and things happen.

4. Killer Apps: Applications are the software that actually do what we need our devices to do. Although we may have hundreds of apps on our phone that can be useful, we regularly use a handful that are critical tools for our daily lives. It is fun to have an app that allows you to point your phone to the sky and it will tell you which constellation you are looking at, but unless you are an astrophysicist, it is probably more important to have an app for making phone calls, sending texts, and checking emails. The whole point of our devices is they can run our killer apps that do what we really need them to do.

THE JESUS REVOLUTION

In some ways the revolutionary movement Jesus began is analogous with this digital revolution. When Jesus came he used the most powerful *programming language* ever developed: the Word of God. It wasn't just that Jesus quoted from the Bible—all the rabbis of his time did that. It was that he quoted and taught from the Bible as a direct representative of his Father, the King of the Universe. And it wasn't only the written Word of God, but it was also the living Word that Jesus heard from the Father directly. This is why people were always amazed at the authority with which he spoke. The binary code of Jesus' programming language was the Word of God understood as both Covenantal relationship and Kingdom representation. It was powerful because it drew people into a personal connection with the God of the Universe and empowered them to act on his behalf.

Likewise, Jesus used this programming language within the *operating system* of discipleship. Although Jesus taught large crowds, his focus was always on the twelve disciples he had chosen and the extended family of disciples who gathered around them. This process of inviting people into a close, personal relationship where they could learn from listening, watching, and participating was central to everything Jesus did. Jesus was intentional about moving his disciples from passive observation to active participation so that in a short time they were trained to do everything he did. This meant they were able to do the same thing with others, making more disciples who in turn could make more disciples. By using the operating system of discipling relationships, Jesus set the stage for an exponential, life-changing movement that could change the world.

One of the extraordinary things about Jesus' teaching and ministry is they were aimed not at the intellectual or spiritual elite but at the ordinary person. Rabbis of Jesus' time typically spoke to other rabbis or their highly trained disciples. By contrast, when Jesus taught he constantly did things like telling simple stories, pointing to flowers in the field and birds overhead, picking up a child, turning over money-changing tables, and myriad other things designed to help ordinary people engage the message he was proclaiming. Jesus used the *GUIs* of his culture to lower the bar and welcome in everyone who wanted to be part of the new Covenant and the coming Kingdom he was inaugurating.

Jesus operated in three primary settings. He invested himself in a small group of disciples, he formed a houseful of people into an extended spiritual family on mission, and he proclaimed the Good News of the Kingdom to large crowds of people. You could say these were the three *killer apps* Jesus uses to produce the church. The small group of twelve disciples allowed him to invest in them at the deepest level and train them to do what he did. The houseful of people formed an extended family that could seek and save the lost and welcome in the broken and hurting. The crowds provided an opportunity to broadcast the transforming message and demonstrate the power of God's presence to as many people as possible. These three killer apps working together ended up forming a movement that literally changed and is still changing the world!

Here's how we might summarize Jesus' methodology using the digital analogy:

1. **Programming Language:** The Word of God understood through both Covenantal relationship and Kingdom representation

2. **Operating System (OS):** Discipleship understood as replicable mentoring relationships

3. **Graphical User Interface (GUI):** Parables, word pictures, physical examples, etc. that helped people connect with his vision and way of life

4. **Killer Apps:** Discipleship in nuclear family (IN), mission in extended family (OUT), and proclamation and demonstration in large public gatherings (UP)

3DM is a movement seeking to follow the Words, Works, and Ways of Jesus. Our approach can be described in very similar terms:

1. **Programming Language:** The Bible read through the lens of Covenant and Kingdom

2. **Operating System (OS):** Discipling relationships that multiply in community

3. **Graphical User Interface (GUI):** Culturally relevant tools such as LifeShapes, matrices, memorable language, etc.

4. **Killer Apps:** Huddles for discipleship (IN), Missional Communities for mission (OUT), and Worship Gatherings for weekly worship (UP)

Scripture is the basis for everything we do, because it is the programming language of Jesus. In reading and listening for the Word of God, we focus on those elements that will bring us into a closer relationship with God and will empower us to more effectively represent him. We believe discipleship is the way we are to do everything. By inviting people into our lives and families, we invest in leaders, equipping them to follow Jesus more closely and do the same with others. We use visual aids and memorable language so everyone can engage with this way of life and pass it on effectively to others. Ultimately, we focus on training leaders to use the key vehicles of Huddle and Missional Community so their churches and organizations will produce more and better Jesus-shaped fruit.[28]

---

28. 3DM does not focus as much on Worship Gatherings because many churches excel in that vehicle already. For related information on worship, see Bob Rognlien, *The Experiential Worshiper* (Torrance: GX Books, 2009) and www.experientialworship.com.

JESUS' BUILDING PROJECT

Ever since Adam and Eve broke Covenant with their Creator by choosing to live life on their own terms, God has been working to redeem and rebuild this broken world into a fruitful Kingdom of joy where his will is done on earth as it is in heaven. Jesus was born into an extended family of builders and stonemasons. At the age of twelve, Jesus was in Jerusalem with his extended family for the Passover. When the rest of the group departed for home, the boy Jesus stayed behind in the Temple courts, unbeknownst to his parents. When they found him there and rebuked him, Luke translates Jesus' reply with an idiomatic Greek phrase that can be translated, *"Did you not know that I must be in my Father's house?"* or *"Did you not know that I must be about my Father's business?"* (Luke 2:49). Even as a boy, Jesus knew his calling was to rebuild the Father's *oikos* so everyone could be part of his family business.

When Jesus invited Peter to join the family business in Caesarea Philippi, he explained how this Kingdom building project would be accomplished: *"I tell you, you are Peter, and on this rock I will build my church, and the gates of hell shall not prevail against it."* (Matthew 16:18) Simon is now Peter, aka Rocky. The implication is obvious: Jesus is not the only Rock in this building project. Jesus' plan to save the world is to use us to build his church. Jesus will do the building if, like Peter and so many others, we will offer our lives to him as the raw material by which God's great rebuilding project is accomplished.

Jesus came to fulfill the Father's business of rebuilding a broken creation. During his last visit to Jerusalem, Jesus predicted the Father was going to carry out

> Jesus operated in three primary settings. He invested himself in a small group of disciples, he formed a houseful of people into an extended spiritual family on mission, and he proclaimed the Good News of the Kingdom to large crowds of people. You could say these were the three *killer apps* Jesus uses to produce the church.

this building project in a very unexpected way by quoting Psalm 118:22: *"Have you never read in the Scriptures: 'The stone that the builders rejected has become the cornerstone; this was the Lord's doing, and it is marvelous in our eyes'?"* (Matthew 21:42). This proved to be a prophetic declaration of how God was going to accomplish his greatest work of all.

Archaeologists have discovered that the rock of Golgotha on which Jesus was crucified is actually a section of limestone that the fifth century BC rebuilders of the Temple quarried around because it was unstable rock, leaving a large rocky outcropping that looked like a skull. The place of Jesus' crucifixion is literally the stone that the builders rejected! On that very rock, Jesus was rejected by those who nailed him to the cross, but through his death and resurrection he has become the cornerstone and has laid the foundation for the Father's work of redemption and restoration. By God's grace now we have the privilege of participating in the completion of this greatest of all building projects.

After many years of seeing Jesus building his church through ordinary people like himself, Peter expressed it this way to his disciples: *"As you come to him, a living stone rejected by men but in the sight of God chosen and precious, you yourselves like living stones are being built up as a spiritual house, to be a holy priesthood, to offer spiritual sacrifices acceptable to God through Jesus Christ."* (1 Peter 2:4-5) Peter had come to understand that empowered missional disciples are the raw material Jesus is using to build a whole new reality.

The word in this phrase we translate spiritual house is literally spiritual *oikos*. We are the living stones Jesus is using to build extended families of disciples whose mission is to seek and save the lost. We are the holy priests called to represent our Father and mediate his saving grace as we welcome the broken and outcast into our spiritual *oikos*, inviting them to follow us as we follow Jesus. We are the means by which Jesus will save the world and establish his eternal Kingdom.

Jesus showed us what this abundant way of life looks like, and he is continuing to build his church by empowering us to live that life today. Like Jesus, we get to decide if we will live as part of our Father's *oikos* and will be about our Father's business. As we embrace our Covenant identity as sons and daughters of the heavenly Father, claiming the authority we have been given to represent our Daddy the King, he will give us the power we need to make disciples the way Jesus did and multiply families on mission who are doing the will of God on earth as it is in heaven. This is God's plan to change the world forever, and we get to be part of it! Jesus is building his church. Our call is simply to empower missional disciples.

YOUR INVITATION

Today followers of Jesus all over the world are part of 3DMovements. We come from varied backgrounds and represent many different tribes. We are part of historic churches, new churches, house churches, megachurches, formal churches, informal churches, city churches, country churches, mission boards, and parachurch organizations. We are seeking to serve and reach people with the Gospel in many different cultural contexts through many different means. But we share a common vision to put Jesus-shaped discipleship back into the hands of ordinary people. We are seeking to build extended missional families that seek and save the lost. We are learning how to carry out this mission in the authority and power of Jesus. Our passion is to empower missional disciples.

If you have resonated with anything in this book, you might be tempted to think that having read it you are now ready to do it in your church.

> Jesus showed us what this abundant way of life looks like, and he is continuing to build his church by empowering us to live that life today. Like Jesus, we get to decide if we will live as part of our Father's *oikos* and will be about our Fahter's business.

That would be to mistake information alone for discipleship! The truth is you can't get discipleship from a book, and you can't give away what you haven't received. We all need someone to imitate before we begin to innovate. Discipleship is a relationship, which means we need to get to know each other. We don't offer any perfect examples of this Way of Jesus, but we do offer living examples and invite you to come follow us as we follow Jesus.

You also might be tempted to think you will be starting Huddles and Missional Communities in your church in the next few months. That would also be a mistake. This is not a program you will implement in a matter of months; it is a new way of life and a culture that will take years to develop. It begins with you, your spouse if you are married, your kids if you have children, people you are close to, those you invite into extended family, and eventually it starts to make an impact on your church as a whole. Those who try to do this on their own inevitably fail, and those who try to rush the process always end up regretting it. Reading this book is the first step in a long journey. Your next step is to meet us so we can start getting to know each other.

If you haven't yet attended a 3DM Discipleship and Mission Workshop, that is the best way to get to know us and find out more. If you have attended a Workshop, we invite you to bring your team and join us for the two-year long 3DM Learning Community training process. This is by far the best resource we offer in implementing the things you have read in this book. If you can't bring a team to a Learning Community, then sign up for an online 3DM Coaching Huddle where you can gain the tools you need to live this out in your daily life and home, at work, and in your neighborhood. For more information visit www.3dmovements.com.

Building a discipling culture and multiplying families on mission is not a quick or easy process, but we have found it is well worth whatever it costs. Jesus said we should count the cost before we answer his call to discipleship. If you feel the Spirit moving you, then come and find out more about what it means to join us on this adventure of empowering missional disciples.